Ron gets you in touch with the many steps to take in order to produce a profitable business.

—Murrell, Oregon

The subject matter, as well as the presentation, was right on target with my expectations and none of my questions were left unanswered.

—John, New Jersey

Having little formal business training and a young company experiencing a 50% growth rate, this program helped us stay in control of our finances.

—Rick, North Carolina

Ron Collier's series of classes has given us the tools to ensure our profitability long-term.

—Dan, Ohio

The Pricing, Costing and Estimating seminar presented by Ron Collier was by far the most informative business seminar I have ever attended.

—Kenneth, Ohio

We are grateful to you for conducting an excellent Financial Management seminar. You've made a significant contribution to our efforts to build a dealer organization.

—Dick, California

Your presentation was another big hit as evidenced by the many wonderful comments we've received since class.

—Todd, Texas

Ron, it was a great symposium. There were many great ideas and techniques presented and I heard nothing but good comments.

—Claude, Texas

I found the material most beneficial to my operation. It could not have come at a better time and I fervently needed your financial "tools" to keep things under control. I wish I had the opportunity to learn your approach fifteen years ago when I started in this business.

—Butch, California

THE STRATEGIES YOU NEED TO OPTIMIZE PROFITS

PROFIT IS AN ATTITUDE

THE STRATEGIES YOU NEED TO OPTIMIZE PROFITS

RON COLLIER, PhD

Supreme Commander
Collier Consulting Group
Austin, TX 78731

AVIVA
PUBLISHING
New York

DEDICATION

To my clients: Thank you for the faith you've all had in me as I helped you in your businesses throughout these 36 years. By attending my seminars, welcoming me into your businesses and using my software, you've continually motivated me to improve and become a better person.

To my wife Sharon: You've encouraged me to go where I would not and have had patience with me in my endeavors for 50 years. Thank you.

ACKNOWLEDGMENTS

I wish to thank the following friends, associates and business partners who have helped me achieve my dreams. If I leave someone out, forgive me. Bill Hanesworth, Tom Nixon, Robert Powell, Brad Bunt, Tom McCart, Joe and Janice Eaton, Nancy Jones, Mark Matteson, Jim Hinshaw, John Abbott, Glenn Taylor, John Androski, Sam Postlethwait, Jim Russell, Al Devito, Robert Hurst, Shari Hastings, Charlie Greer, David Holt and Richard Harshaw.

I would also like to thank Patrick Snow for his support and coaching. His mentorship helped me avoid so many first-timer mistakes. Special thanks to my editor Sara Keeney. Her guidance through my manuscript was incredible.

CONTENTS

Preface   21

Introduction   25
  Three Hats

Chapter 1: Mastering the Right Attitude   33
  Take a Look in the Mirror
  Develop a Profit Attitude
  Inspire With Your Attitude
  Know Who You Work For
  Hire the Right Attitude
  Summary

Chapter 2: Trying to Be All Things to All People   43
  Don't Be All Things to All People
  Hire a Hat
  Summary

Chapter 3: Paving the Way to Profits   51
  Follow the Right Order
    Finances
    Marketing
    Selling
  Choose the Right Software
    Accounting Software
    Customer Management Software
  Choose the Right Accounting Firm
  Get Started With Finances

Profit & Loss Statements

Summary

Chapter 4: Measuring Growth   **71**

Balance Sheet

   Assets

   Liabilities

   Net Worth

Summary

Chapter 5: Making Your Money Work for You   **87**

Choose Cash or Credit

Understand Working Capital

Working Capital Turnover (WCTO)

   Over-Capitalized

   Under-Capitalized

Summary

Chapter 6: Breaking Even Is Better Than Losing   **97**

Breakeven Formula

Summary

Chapter 7: Getting a Return on Your Investment   **103**

Return on Investment (ROI)

Return on Investment Calculations

Return on Investment and Budgeting

Summary

Chapter 8: Evaluating Your Success   **111**

Short-Term Ratios

Current Ratio

Quick Ratio

Gross Margin Ratio

Net Margin Ratio

Cash Conversion Cycle Elements

Inventory Turn-Days

Accounts Receivables Turn-Days

Average Payment Period Days

Cash Conversion Cycles

Equity and Asset Ratios

Sales to Assets Ratio

Return on Assets Ratio

Return on Equity (Net Worth)

Debt to Equity Ratio

Working Capital Turnover Ratio

Electronic Financial Officer (eFO)

Summary

Chapter 9: Pricing For Profit   **125**

Volume and Price-Sensitive Businesses

Volume-Sensitive Businesses

Price-Sensitive Businesses

Pricing Strategies

Strategic Market Pricing

Strategic Pricing Strategies

Gross Margin Method

Dual Overhead Allocation Method

Flat Rate Pricing for Service and Installation Companies

Summary

Chapter 10: Collecting Your Profits   **147**

Cash Flow

Accounts Receivables Aging

Summary

Chapter 11: Controlling Costs   **159**

Types of Costs

    Direct

    Indirect Variable Overhead

    Indirect Fixed Overhead

Controlling Direct Costs

    Suppliers

    Inventory Control

    Labor

    Other Direct Costs

Controlling Indirect Variable Overhead

    Advertising

    Auto and Truck Maintenance

    Auto and Truck Gas and Oil

    Bad Debts

    Equipment Expense

    Freight

    Interest and Bank Charges

    Miscellaneous

    Office Expenses

    Payroll Taxes

Sales Commissions

Shop Supplies and Tools

Travel and Entertainment

Unapplied Labor

Unapplied Materials

Vacation, Holiday and Bonus Pay

Controlling Indirect Fixed Overhead

Advertising

Employee Benefits

Owner's Salary

Summary

Chapter 12: Creating Customers for Life   **185**

Understand Marketing Verses Advertising

Use the Customers for Life Model (CFL)

Develop Your Plan

Get Out

Generate Leads

Manage Customer Files

Summary

Chapter 13: Organizing for Success   **199**

Add Names to Your Organizational Chart

Create Profit Centers

Summary

Chapter 14: Hiring Right the First Time   **205**

Write Job Descriptions

Interview Effectively

Pre-Hire
Develop a Procedure Manual
Manage Goals
Manage Time
    Time Coming & Going
    Management Time
Follow the Rules When De-Hiring
Summary

Chapter 15: Franchising Your Business   **217**
Sell Consistency
Create Systems Like a Franchise Does
Create Procedures
Track Employees
Summary

Chapter 16: Planning Your Future   **225**
Be Profitable
Create Your Budget
Make Money in One of Three Ways
Summary

A Final Note   235
Glossary   241
Bibliography   249
Appendix   257
About the Author   273
About Ron Collier Consulting   275
About Ron Collier Coaching   277
Book Ron Collier To Speak at Your Next Event   279

PREFACE

didn't wake up one day and decide to write a book, but the pandemic of 2020 was a prime motivator, and it gave me the time I needed. In 1984 I began working with small businesses. What I found interesting was that businesses looked alike, regardless of size, and they had very similar problems. They moved from one-man shops to businesses to large organizations but along the way they all had to overcome the same hurdles to grow successfully.

If you're a business owner, you'll fall in one of three categories of business: small, medium or large.

- Small businesses typically do $0–$300k in sales.
- Medium businesses do $300–800k in sales.
- Large businesses do over $800k.

Businesses move through phases of growth, plateau and hopefully, more growth. All businesses have a plateau or growth wall that many can't scale. For a business to grow, it must move over the wall, which sometimes requires tough decisions.

The main reason I wrote this book is because I have observed thousands of businesses and found that most of them are stuck behind the growth wall. To be successful, you must be willing to accept the work involved in getting over the wall, have the passion to be profitable and implement the strategies I outline in this book. Without profit, nothing in a business works. So, that's my number one goal: to make you money.

This book will teach you the keys to running a profitable business. No giant chapters on selling or marketing, no fluff, no generic platitudes. Instead we'll focus on what you need to know in order to be profitable. Every business is different, and every business owner has different needs, but making a profit is a requirement for every single business and every single business owner.

In this book I'll tell you what to do and how to do it. Good luck—I wish you the very best on your journey.

INTRODUCTION

*"Profit in business comes from repeat customers,
customers that boast about your project or service,
and that bring friends with them."*

—*William Deming*

Owning a small business isn't as fun as you expected it to be. You work long hours and aren't able to spend the time you want with your family. You never seem to make enough to get ahead. You're starting to think that you'll never be able to sock away some money. You've been through too many employees to count. Retirement is just a dream. You're surviving week-to-week.

Exercise

Answer the questions below by circling yes or no.

Do you have to go to work every day to open the office?
Yes   No

Do you have enough money to retire and sell the business?

Yes   No

Can you take off work to spend time with your family?
Yes   No

Do you really enjoy your 12-hour-a-day job?

Yes   No

If you answered *no* to any of these, your small business is making your life miserable. I know what it's like to work 12 hours per day, six to seven days a week and feel like you're not any better off for all that effort. Life in a small business should be better for you because you're the one in control, not someone else.

This book was written for you because I feel your pain. Business owners like you are technicians, managers and entrepreneurs. You have incredible expertise, but you may not have much in-depth knowledge about:

- Solid accounting that will keep you on the right track and show you if you're profitable

- Effective cash flow management so you can always pay the bills

- Useful metrics that can show you how you compare to your industry

- Strategic pricing and working capital management that will put you in a profitable position and outpace your competitors

- Detailed analysis of every element of your business so that you focus internally instead of externally

If you're dedicated to your small business and have the passion to succeed, this book will give you the insights, strategies, skills, knowledge and metrics to be a *profitable* business, not just a business.

I started my small business in August of 1991. I was already tired of my job at a major manufacturer when I got the "entrepreneurial seizure."

Michael Gerber, author of *E-Myth Revisited*, describes the entrepreneurial seizure perfectly in his *Inc.* article from 2016: *It's when a person excels in a particular area of expertise and thinks, therefore, that he or she could run a successful business that does that work.*

I came home after work that month and told my wife that I was quitting my corporate job (the one with great pay, benefits, vacation and a 401k) because I got the "seizure." It wasn't my fault! The seizure made me do it!

My beautiful wife reminded me that my son was starting his freshmen year at the University of Texas in Austin and my daughter was starting her junior year of high school at the Texas Academy of Math & Science at the University of North Texas. The seizure answered, "no problem." I quit my job the following Monday.

But my entrepreneurial seizure was a smart one. Many months before that fateful date in 1991, I had already begun to research going out on my own, reading countless books on the subject. I even lined up a lot of clients before I quit my job, so I didn't go from riches to rags. I had enough confidence in myself, as well as the swagger and the attitude, to succeed. I didn't "hope to succeed," but instead, I made success a mandatory goal. The only person responsible for my paycheck was me and I couldn't fail myself or my family.

I had started helping companies improve their bottom line back in 1984 when I was hired into the training department of a major corporation. Their customers were mostly service-oriented businesses, but many also had retail shops. Like most businesses, the companies I worked with made enough money to survive, but they had little left over to invest in, or grow, the business. Even those with extra money didn't know how to spend it properly.

When you go into business for yourself, you must be careful that you don't hold the same job as you did before. If you do, then you just have a different boss.

Three Hats

As Michael Gerber points out in his book, most businesses fail because they don't have the time to:

- Grow the business (entrepreneur)
- Manage the business (manager)
- Provide the product or service that the customer hired them for (technician)

Nearly all business owners try to wear all three hats. Therefore, businesses fail because of a lack of focus on what the owner needs to do.

What is your strength? What should your role in the company be? You can't be all things to all people.

I found out soon enough that what most business owners wanted to do was market, sell and get more customers. I've had to explain many times that sometimes the worst things you can do are market and sell. Why would you want to sell more items if your prices aren't set properly, you don't have the right personnel, you don't have enough product and your costs are out of control? If you're losing money, you would only be speeding up the process of failure.

It's important to remember why you went into business for yourself in the first place. You quit your job because:

- You wanted to grow your business, and then, as you neared retirement, sell it for a handsome profit.
- You wanted to make more money.
- You wanted to have more free time to spend with your family.

If you're working more than 40 hours per week and have less time to spend with your family and friends than you did when you were employed elsewhere, this book is for you.

If you're not making a lot more money than you did at your previous job, this book is for you.

If you've been in business for several years and have a negative (or low) net worth, this book is for you.

If your business can't pay its bills, this book is for you.

This book was written to show business owners how to use the financial information they already have to make intelligent decisions that will grow the business. All businesses have highs and lows, but great businesses continue to move forward in spite of the owner's shortcomings, overcoming obstacles in the marketplace and surpassing the competition.

I was fortunate enough to earn a PhD from Purdue University, where I learned (theoretically) what small businesses need to do to succeed. However, it's working with thousands of businesses over the last 30 years that taught me exactly why and how business owners should implement the changes I suggest in this book.

All businesses go through many of the same phases that humans do: infancy, childhood, the teen years and adulthood. We all experience the same basic needs and desires during the phases of our lives, but how we achieve these basic needs and desires differs based on our environment. In my workshops, I teach pricing to companies valued at $10 million and companies valued at $1 million. How does that work? I teach basic concepts that can be applied to meet the different needs of each and every company.

I wrote this book to give you the basics needed to succeed in business. This book will show you how to develop a plan, but you'll need someone to review that plan and offer suggestions and alternative paths to success. I can become your coach and mentor, guiding you over the finish line. I've never seen a business fail because of a lack of customers or sales. Businesses fail because of poor management.

Give me the chance to change the way you do business.

If you're ready, I'm sure ready. Now is the time, so turn the page.

CHAPTER 1

MASTERING THE RIGHT ATTITUDE

"There are always opportunities through which businesses can profit handsomely if they only recognize and seize them."

—*Jean Paul Getty*

S uccess comes from good management. Failure comes from bad management. Attitude, however, is at the core of both good and bad management.

Webster defines attitude as: *a bodily state of readiness to respond in a characteristic way to a stimulus (such as an object, concept or situation).* The way you approach the situations that will occur in your business every day will determine your future.

Take a Look in the Mirror

I remember being called to evaluate a company. As I do with all eval-

uations, I asked the owner to not ask me any questions until the evaluation was over and I had all the facts.

On the third night, as I shared a meal with the owner and his wife, he asked, "Well, have you found the problem?"

Reluctantly I said, "Yes, it's you. You have great managers and employees in key positions. They're making money for you...until you come in and stir the pot. You have key people making good decisions. Starting tomorrow, I don't want you to go to the office until after 10 a.m. By that time, decisions will have been made and you can't change the day. Have breakfast with your wife, go golfing, go to a meeting and let your employees make you money."

That's always a tough conversation, but this business owner's attitude toward his employees—and his need to do everything his way—would be the thing that caused him to fail. Your greatest liability is in the mirror, so take notice.

Develop a Profit Attitude

So many businesses struggle to be successful. A successful company is one that can take care of the owner, employees and customers while still making a profit. If a company can't make a true profit and the owner and employees aren't rewarded for their service, the company fails.

You've probably heard more than one business owner say, "I don't take a salary. I just put all the money back into the business."

I find this completely astonishing. Who pays their personal expenses? Is the business just an expensive hobby? Is someone else paying the bills? If I'm a business owner and my company doesn't pay me a salary, why am I working such long hours when I could be working for someone else just 40 hours per week?

It's attitude and fortitude that will make or break a business. As a small business owner, you need a profit attitude. This means you go to work and make the correct choices to make a profit. You must be in the right mindset to make money.

Exercise

Do you wake up in the morning and have profit as your mandatory goal or do you wake up and hope to make money?

How many hours per week do you want to work?

How many hours per week do you need to work?

Is there a difference between the two? If so, why?

Let's make this crystal clear: If you don't want to make money, earn a profit and grow your business, there's no need to waste your time and energy or the time and energy of others involved in the business. You should enter your business through the profit door each day and stay in the profit room until closing.

Think about it this way: How many diet plans do you need to follow to lose weight? How many smoking cessation programs do you need to participate in to quit smoking? One, and only one, so long as you have the right attitude and the right plan to follow.

Inspire With Your Attitude

I was fortunate to study under a great scholar, Sam Postlethwait, at Purdue University. I say fortunate because not only was he my major professor, he was my mentor and the person I aspired to become. His attitude was inspiring.

Dr. Postlethwait made it a point to learn the name of each of his students—and with over 1,200 students, that was no small feat!

He started each semester by getting a list of the names of the students he would have in class. Then, upon meeting each student, he'd shake their hand and look them in the eye, asking, "What is your first name?"

"My name is Mary," the student would reply, for example.

He would then ask the name of the next student, go back to the previous student and say, "Mary, I would like for you to meet Sam."

When the next student, John, revealed his name, Dr. Postlethwait would introduce Mary and Sam to John.

"John, I would like you to meet Mary. John, I would like you to meet Sam."

He would continue around the room of over 200 students, repeating each name over and over. He was determined to get every name right.

At the end of the exercise, he would ask the class if anyone would like to introduce the entire class. At least 10 or more would raise their hands, and many of them—those who were truly inspired by the professor's attitude—were successful.

In classes large and small, I witnessed Dr. Postlethwait establish a rapport with his students over and over. His attitude showed a drive to learn and it was contagious. In one 50-minute period, this professor earned the respect of his students, which continued throughout the semester.

Great business owners have—and keep—the right attitude, which is then passed down to their employees. Most employees know when a business is barely surviving, and the great employees will move on. They don't want to work with a company that doesn't do the right things to make a profit.

Exercise

How do you make your attitude transferable to your employees?

Do you believe attitudes change with age, time or social awareness? If so, how do they change?

For many years I taught a great small business development class to individuals who owned, or were thinking about starting, their own business. Different professionals led sections on financing, marketing, payroll, taxes, etc. I kicked off the class by providing the students with an outline of what it takes to be successful. Time and time again we talked about what it takes to start a business.

I discovered that many in the class really wanted a hobby that would make them money. Don't get me wrong, I love my hobby of fishing, but having a hobby that you love and starting a business to make money are miles apart.

Many in the class just wanted to know if any banks or the Small Business Administration (SBA) would give them money to try to start a business. They felt no personal responsibility and wanted the bank to give them 100% of the funds needed to start and the SBA to guarantee the loan if they could not make the payments. They had the desire to start a company, but not the right attitude, nor the personal responsibility, to succeed.

One business owner had a negative profit of over $40,000. He spent more than $9,000 on video cameras to capture inventory "theft" and over $60,000 cash to buy a new truck. I don't think his attitude was in the right place.

Exercise

How much profit as a percent of sales do you want to retain in your company after you've paid all your expenses, including your salary (and your significant other's salary, if they're employed with you)?

Why do you need to make a profit in addition to your normal salary? Why is profit important?

Know Who You Work For

Every day you need to remember who you work for and focus on making the company successful. When you own a small business, you have a responsibility to:

- Yourself
- Your family
- Your employees
- Your customers

This focus on success is mandatory. If you don't want to make money and don't want to create a business that can sustain itself, then get out of the business before you're forced out.

Your customers and employees will observe your attitude and your employees will mimic how you act. If you don't dress appropriately, your employees won't dress appropriately. If you aren't respectful to customers, your employees won't be respectful to customers.

Hire the Right Attitude

Hire on attitude first, then skills. When you hire new employees, which we'll cover at length in Chapter 14, base it on how they communicate, how they dress, how they act and how they respond to your questions. You can teach skills, but you can't teach attitude. Attitude has been established over decades. If an employee isn't a "morning person" for example, you'll not change that fact. If an attitude changes, it's usually the result of an extreme situation.

Summary

If you go to work every day with the right attitude and mindset, you can change lives.

I joined the Scouts at the age of eight. My goal was to be the best I could be and to achieve the rank of Eagle Scout in high school. I was earning all the needed merit badges for Eagle, but swimming was my greatest challenge. You see, my mother never learned to swim and she just knew she would die if she got near the water. She instilled that attitude in me and I'd get panic attacks if even my bath water was too deep! Water was death to me, and I feared and avoided it.

By the time I reached high school, I had just two merit badges left to earn to become an Eagle Scout—Swimming and Lifesaving. My father was a leader in Scouts and I asked him if I could become an Eagle Scout any other way. The answer was no—there would be no exceptions on the path to Eagle Scout. If you didn't learn to swim and get that merit badge, and then go on to get the Lifesaving badge, you could not become an Eagle Scout.

My passion for the Eagle Scout award overcame my fear of water. Slowly, over three months that summer, I learned to swim. At 16 years old, it was one of the hardest things I had ever done, but I had to change my attitude about water to achieve success.

Understand that not only are you providing for others today, but you're growing a business that you'll be able to sell. Your business is your investment in time and money, and that investment can be rewarded in the future.

CHAPTER 2:

TRYING TO BE ALL THINGS TO ALL PEOPLE

"An entrepreneur builds an enterprise; a technician builds a job."

—*Michael Gerber*

I believe that the best book series ever written for small business is the *E-Myth* by Michael Gerber. I suggest that all business owners read that book from front to back, then back to front. It's really that good. Even though Michael Gerber has written several books, the revised *The E-Myth Revisited* is his best. This book not only explains the myth, but how to overcome it.

The *E-Myth* basically says that starting your own business to become an entrepreneur is a myth. When you start a business, you may think that you're an entrepreneur—and your friends will be impressed that you took the leap and went into business—but the premise isn't correct.

When you're working for someone else you wear one hat, but when you start a business you wear three hats. When you start your own business, you're not just the entrepreneur who gets the work. You're also the technician who does the work and the manager who controls the work.

Why do most businesses fail? Because the owner is trying to wear all three hats, but their head isn't big enough. Oh, it swells and takes on all the hats, but they keep falling off. No one owner can do successfully what must be done by three players.

Don't Be All Things to All People

Consider a baker. A baker works for a bakery until one day she gets the "entrepreneurial seizure." She decides to start her own bakery and become an entrepreneur. She can't stand for her creativity to be thwarted by her current boss for one more second!

She finds a facility, she moves in and she starts doing what she knows how to do—bake. She bakes…and bakes…and then bakes some more…but she never seems to have the time to manage the books or bring in more customers. She thinks she's an entrepreneur, but she's actually just a baker who sees her new boss when she looks in the mirror.

Now let's consider an air conditioning and heating service technician. He leaves the company he's been at for 10 years to go out on his own. I mean, he really knows what he's doing at this point, right?

He buys a truck, he gets some tools and he starts by doing work for his friends. Pretty soon he's working 60 hours per week, answering his phone seven days per week and losing money. He doesn't have the time to be the technician, manager and entrepreneur. He'll probably be able to pay his bills, but he'll never have a successful, sustainable company.

Many small companies with three to five employees fall into this trap—and they never get out. The owner won't let go. He's too busy losing money. He's the hamster inside the wheel to nowhere.

Exercise

Why do you have to do everything yourself?

Are you willing to transfer all your cell phone calls to an office phone for someone else to answer?

Will you allow someone else to schedule your appointments and talk to customers?

I got a call from a business owner late on a Friday night. After confirming that I was, in fact, a qualified business consultant, he poured his heart out. At 68 years old, he had been a plumber for over 35 years. He had done the majority of the work himself. His sons helped him out part-time and his wife helped when she could, but he was at the point where he couldn't pay his bills and he couldn't care for his family. Even though he worked 12 hours per day 6 days per week, he couldn't meet his obligations and the bank was closing in.

This plumber was so busy wearing his plumber hat, he didn't have time for the manager hat or the entrepreneur hat. He was busy, but his business didn't grow and he was barely surviving. He had virtually no assets and few customers. There was no business; the business and the owner were the same. If this business owner got out of the business, the business would cease to exist.

The problem with being—and staying—a technician is that you don't own a business, the business owns you. You don't have a company, you just have one person. No company is formed. If the technician is hurt or dies, the company dies too.

Think about it this way: If you're a technician entrepreneur, your spouse or significant other is just one heartbeat away from owning a company.

Hire a Hat

The owner must wear the technician's hat first but move toward wearing only the entrepreneur hat.

When the technician lays his tools on the shelf and leaves them there, when the baker hangs up her apron and doesn't put it back on, a company has been formed. The technician and the baker are now CEOs of sustainable organizations.

My workshop attendees always say that they can't afford to hire someone, or they say that they just want to stay small. That decision is personal but realize that in those cases you'll never have a company to sell and you'll never be able to make the money you desire. Companies make money collectively from employees and the owner. If you're making all the money for the company by being a technician and you never hire and manage employees or go after new work, you'll never grow or achieve your dreams.

Hire a full-time office person to take the manager's hat and handle things like accounting, dispatching, talking with customers and scheduling appointments. You'll be amazed at how much time it frees up so that you can start to put on your entrepreneur hat once in a while.

I know you're probably thinking, "I can't afford it. I can barely pay the bills now." You have no choice. You must get rid of at least one hat and the manager's hat is typically the one that doesn't fit well. You don't have time to do the manager's job, so give that hat away. Borrow the money, take out a home improvement loan, develop a profit attitude and do what you must do. You'll be surprised by how much more business you can do when you have the time and opportunity to network as an entrepreneur.

Exercise

What must I do now to hire the person who will wear the manager hat?

Once you've grown the business, hire a technician as soon as possible so that you can take off the technician hat too. When you start working *on* your business instead of working *in* your business, the money will flow.

Summary

The *E-Myth* tells us how to properly start and grow a business. It offers guidance, but you as the owner must make the correct choices. You can't be everything to everyone. It's impossible for one person to do what is required of a technician, manager and entrepreneur. You must give up some control in order to grow your business.

CHAPTER 3

PAVING THE WAY TO PROFITS

*"The difference between winning and
losing is most often not quitting."*

—*Walt Disney*

This book focuses on understanding the profitable side of business. Once you've got that under control, you can make intelligent choices on finances, marketing and selling. In this chapter, we'll look at each of those and then move on to the basic tools you'll need: accounting software, customer management software and an accounting team. We'll conclude with the first financial component of your business, the profit & loss statement.

Follow the Right Order

All businesses, regardless of their product or service, must focus on three things in order to be successful:

1. Finances
2. Marketing
3. Selling

If these are out of order, chaos and business failure ensues.

Finances

The first thing you focus on is the financial side of your business, whether you're starting a new business or jump-starting an existing business with a re-grand opening. The financial side of business is the focus of this book.

The finances associated with your business determine the costs, sales, budgets, profitability, salaries and wages that must be used to determine the pricing for your products and services.

You must be able to produce monthly profit & loss and balance sheets, and you must analyze both monthly (see Appendix for sample Electronic Financial Officer (eFO) described in Chapter 8) so you know every 30 days whether you're making or losing money. Don't wait until the end of the year or quarter to find out because by then it's too late to do anything about it. If you focus and make money monthly, I can assure you that your year will turn out fine.

Marketing

Let's be clear: this isn't a book on marketing. You need to get your financial house in order before you convince anyone to buy from you.

Only after you can produce and analyze the financial information from your business, which allows you to price your products and services correctly, can you move up the pyramid to marketing.

Marketing is everything that you say and do to convince customers that buying from you is the right decision. If you're good at marketing, selling is easy and there will be few price objections.

Develop a definitive marketing plan with a Customers for Life (see Chapter 12) mentality at its core. Market to all types of customers every day, spend most of your money on existing customers and network, network, network.

Selling

Once you've priced your products and services correctly and developed a great marketing plan, you can move up the pyramid to selling.

If you've instilled the right value into your products and services, the customer should already be in the right frame of mind to purchase. If a customer perceives a higher value than your sale price, you've locked in the sale.

Choose the Right Software

Computer literacy is a must when you start a business and choosing the right accounting or point of sale (POS) software is critical. I bring up the need for both accounting and customer management software packages to make you more aware of your customers and their value to you.

Online software programs are sometimes not as powerful as desktop programs. And you may find that you don't have the bandwidth; the programs may timeout due to your internet or wireless connection. In addition, what happens to your data if you decide to transition to a different provider? They have a history of all your transactions and data, but where is it? What format is it in? How do you save it or transition it to another program?

Wireless interaction with the field is great, but it isn't the utopia of doing business. Do your homework and find the answers before you invest. Be sure to ask:

- Is the system going to capture the information that you need from the customer?
- Will the data integrate into your accounting package?
- Will all of the data collected be integrated, or only some of the data?

Be sure that you have the answers to these and other questions before you commit long-term.

Accounting Software

You'll want to use accounting software, not a check register, to track expenses and sales. Accounting software will allow you to produce the financial documents that you need to review monthly to track your company's progress, notably the profit & loss statement and the balance sheet.

Balance Sheet: The balance sheet shows the value of your business from the first day of operation. You've done one of two things since you opened your doors: made money or lost money. The balance sheet will show you if you're moving up or down.

Profit & Loss Statement (P&L): The profit & loss statement shows the results of sales activities monthly, quarterly, yearly or longer. It shows your sales revenue, your costs of those sales and overhead expenses.

Accounting software, like QuickBooks, Netsuite or Sage, allows you to easily track expenditures, bill customers and pay your bills. You'll know immediately how much your customers owe you and how much you owe. It's also useful for tracking inventory and determining the exact costs of running your business.

Customer Management Software

Customer management software will give you a complete history of the products, service and maintenance for each customer in one spot.

Do you have that ability now or do you have to look at multiple paper files housed in physical filing cabinets? No one wants to purchase an unorganized company, so you need to make sure that your valuable customer data is easily accessible and useable.

Software like ACT!, GoldMine, Salesforce, Constant Contact or CallProof tracks all customer activities including sales calls, telephone calls, email, sales volume and key contacts. CallProof (callproof.com) offers a great mobile customer relationship management (CRM) package. Many packages will also allow you to dispatch or send orders directly to your field personnel.

If you're a service-oriented company, you might consider Field Edge (DESCO) or Davisware (WINTAC) for mobile solutions and Sage100/300 if you do a lot of commercial projects or new construction. If you run a retail store, look for the point of sale (POS) package that best suits your industry.

You do need both accounting and customer management software to be successful. Accounting software can tell you if a customer owes you money, but it can't give you the specifics of why that money is owed or provide a history of the customer's relationship with your company. It's the customer management software that tells you when a call was taken, who went on the call, the serial number of the equipment repaired or if the equipment is under warranty.

Choose the Right Accounting Firm

There are several services and qualifications to consider when searching for an accounting firm. Here's what I look for:

Qualifications

☐ Accounting experience through college, university or continuing education classes

☐ Reference list of small business clients, preferably some similar to your company

☐ Experience in accounting and tax work in your specific industry

☐ Professional support staff that can answer your questions

☐ Few (never zero) tax audits from returns they have done

☐ Certification through a state or local agency that requires audits, evaluations and training of accounting firms (i.e. CPAs)

Services

- ☐ Help prepare monthly profit & loss statement and balance sheet
- ☐ Help prepare payroll in a timely manner, plus file payroll reports to state agencies
- ☐ Review your internal accounting procedures and recommend changes to coordinate efforts
- ☐ Prepare quarterly payroll/income tax reports
- ☐ Provide tax planning advice before and during each tax year to maximize legitimate business deductions and develop strategies for both personal and business gain of income/deductions
- ☐ Review local, state and federal compliance laws that impact your company
- ☐ Recommend computer programs that are specific to your company
- ☐ Meet with you and other relevant team members quarterly to evaluate the business, advise on the direction of the company and personal goals, provide guidance on tax strategies

The costs of these services can depend upon your locale and how complicated your tax situation. Costs could range from $100 to over $1,000 or more per month depending upon the types of services you require. You'll get what you pay for, so you should establish a value of the accounting office as related to price.

It's important to note that an accounting firm may or not be your best tax firm. Do you need someone to guide you through proper accounting methods or do it all for you? Is the person who handles your accounting or bookkeeping also your tax person? Be sure that the individuals handling both are qualified for the things you need done.

It's important to have a great accountant in your corner who can also represent you in front of the IRS. Most businesses are led by good salespeople, installers or technicians, but not many are led by accounting people. Help yourself and your business by hiring an accounting firm that will become your trusted business advisor. This is one area of your business that you don't want to ignore or hedge on price.

Get Started With Finances

Profit & Loss Statements

The profit & loss statement is like the speedometer on your car. It shows how quickly or slowly you're reaching your destination: profitability.

I asked the participants in one of my classes to bring in the most recent profit & loss statement for their business. About 30% of the students didn't have one and one student brought three boxes of bank statements and a checkbook. When running a small business, it's imperative to do accounting, not checking. Don't run your company out of a checkbook. Run your company through computer software that tracks all sales and expenses. Use this software to produce both profit & loss and balance sheets. To run a profitable company, you must be organized and know when you're making or losing money. Checkbooks can't do that.

Your accountant and eFO (Chapter 8 and Appendix) will help you analyze your financial data. I've provided a sample profit & loss statement (Appendix) with key categories for all businesses, including service businesses. In this book I'll show you what I think is most important on the profit & loss statement.

You need to produce a profit & loss statement at the end of each month or by the fifth of the next month. You need to look at the statement monthly to determine if you're making money. Many small businesses only look at their profit & loss at the end of the year and by then it's too late. I want you to run your business monthly—and I don't mean starting next month or one month next year. Starting now, focus on making money this month. Then repeat, repeat, repeat...

The profit & loss statement is divided into six areas that need your attention monthly:

1. Sales revenue
2. Cost of goods sold
3. Gross margin (GM) or gross profit
4. Variable overhead
5. Fixed overhead
6. Net profit before taxes (NPBT)

Profit and Loss Statement Worksheet

		$	%	TARGET
SALES				
	Wholesale			
	Retail			
Total Sales				
	Cost of Materials			
	Cost of Equipment			
	Cost of Labor			
	Cost of Subcontractor			
	Cost of Warranty			
	Other Costs			
Total Direct Costs				
GROSS MARGIN				

Sales Revenue

Sales revenue is the total income to the company through normal sales activities.

As you record your sales revenue, you may want to track where the revenue is generated and by whom. The more information about the sale, the better the tracking and the better the accounting output.

I asked one of my clients how many employees he had in his company. He replied, "22." I asked how many of those were salespeople and he replied, "22."

Revenue is recorded through cash accounting or accrual accounting.

Cash accounting only records revenue received. Most retail establishments who get paid immediately through cash, check or credit card use cash accounting.

Other businesses, like service businesses who bill customers, use accrual accounting.

Accrual accounting records revenue received and unreceived. Accrual accounting is the most accurate, but regardless of which method is chosen, print your profit & loss statements on the accrual basis to get the best data.

Costs of Goods Sold (COGS)

Cost of goods sold is sometimes called direct cost or job costs.

Cost of goods sold records the specific costs of doing jobs.

For a cost to go into this category, it must match with a sale. For example, if I sell a bicycle for $400 and the cost of the materials used to make the bicycle are $200, the $200 materials cost should go in cost of goods sold. The cost and sale are tied to each other. However, electricity for my bike shop can't go in this category because I can't tie the cost of electricity to the sale of the bike. It would be difficult, if not impossible, to say that I used $1.47 in electricity to sell the bike.

Costs tied directly to a job go into cost of goods sold, other costs go into overhead or administrative expenses.

Also, note that this category is costs of goods *sold*—it isn't cost of goods *bought*. Don't skip inventory control and put all purchases here. That would give you an incorrect value, since it would also include cost of goods bought. You only include items moved out of inventory when they are sold. We'll discuss how to handle your inventory in a later chapter.

Subcategories of cost of goods sold include:

- Materials
- Equipment
- Subcontractors
- Warranty
- Other
- Field labor

We look at these differently depending upon if you own a retail business or a service business.

Materials are the costs of inventory with no serial number. In a service business like heating, ventilation and air conditioning or plumbing, this would include copper pipe, toilets, sinks, etc. In a retail business, this would include the cost of the inventory sold, not bought.

Equipment is the costs of inventory with a serial number. In a service business like heating, ventilation and air conditioning or plumbing, this would include air conditioners, furnaces, water heaters, etc. In a retail business, it might include tractors, lawn mowers or automobiles.

If the inventory item has a specific number to differentiate it, it's equipment. If the item only has a date code showing the date manufactured, and there's no serial number to differentiate it, it goes in materials.

Subcontractors are the companies that you hire to do work for you. They aren't employees, they are outside help. If you can tie their cost to a specific job, the cost goes here. If you can't, the cost goes into overhead as contract labor or temporary help.

Use caution with subcontractors. Many businesses today try to pass their employees off as subcontractors and they've gotten into trouble. Be sure that subcontractors bill you, you don't pay them in cash and you file a 1099 with the IRS for their work.

Warranty costs are the costs tied to a manufacturer's warranty. These are the costs you incur in taking care of the warranty for the manufacturer. You may or may not be reimbursed for these costs, but they're still tied to a job.

Other costs are those miscellaneous direct costs that can also be tied to a job. Examples include buying a permit or renting a crane for a job.

Field labor costs are the wages you pay to field personnel that can be billed to a job. These wages could include service technicians, plumbers, landscapers or swimming pool repair persons.

If you pay an employee $30 per hour and they work 2 hours repairing a furnace at Ms. Smith's house, those wages go here because you can bill the time spent on the repair to Ms. Smith.

If you can't tie time to a specific job, the wage goes in overhead instead.

Labor is one of your greatest expenses and we discuss it at length in Chapter 11.

Gross Margin or Gross Profit

The difference between sales revenue and costs of goods sold is gross margin.

I prefer the term gross margin over gross profit because I don't want it to be confused with net profit.

Gross margin is an important number for businesses and it's a strong measurement tool. This number shows you the money that you have left over after paying all direct job costs. That leftover money is what pays for overhead and profit. The higher the margin the better because it means that you're controlling your jobs.

Exercise

Where do temporary office personnel wages go on the profit & loss statement?

Would cost of inventory go under cost of goods sold?

Profit and Loss Statement Worksheet	$	%	TARGET
OPERATING EXPENSES			
Variable Overhead			
Advertising			
Vehicle Gas and Oil			
Vehicle Repair and Maintenance			
Bad Debits			
Equipment Expenses			
Freight			
Interest and Bank Charges			
Insurance (Work Comp/General Liability)			
Office Expenses			
Payroll Taxes			
Sales Commissions			
Shop Supplies and Tools			
Travel and Entertainment			
Unapplied Labor			
Unapplied Materials			
Vacation, Holiday and Bonus Pay			
Total Variable Overhead			

Variable Overhead

Variable overhead items on a profit & loss statement are items that relate to jobs indirectly.

Typical variable overhead categories include automobile repair, maintenance and gas bills, payroll taxes, workers compensation and general liability insurance, and turn on/off marketing expenses.

These costs support sales but aren't directly related to them. If you stopped selling tomorrow, most all costs of goods sold and variable overhead would disappear.

While many companies don't separate their overhead into variable and fixed, it's important to do so. By separating them, you can figure your breakeven value for sales and also know which costs must be paid.

Profit and Loss Statement Worksheet	$	%	TARGET
Fixed Overhead			
Advertising			
Communication			
Contributions			
Data Processing			
Depreciation			
Dues and Subscriptions			
Employee Benefits			
Legal and Professional Fees			
Licenses and Taxes			
Repair and Maintenance			
Rent Expense			
Salaries - Office			
Salaries - Officer			
Salaries - Supervisory			
Salaries - Warehouse			
Uniforms and Laundry			
Utilities			
Total Fixed Overhead			
Total Overhead Expenses			
Net Profit Before Taxes			

Fixed Overhead

These may be expenses you have to pay even if you're not selling anything.

Fixed overhead could include rent, fixed marketing expenses, lease payments for vehicles, office salaries, utilities and phones. These expenses are typically fixed and don't change much as sales change.

Your salary and your significant other's salary, if they are involved in the business, also go in fixed overhead. The first check you write each week is to yourself and the second is to your significant other. Why own a company that pays you last? Why suffer through all the stress and long hours and not get paid? Let's look at a typical scenario:

One of my clients in Alabama didn't take a salary. His wife was a schoolteacher and provided the family with the necessary income and insurance.

The husband worked in the business and didn't receive a paycheck or benefits.

The wife did the accounting for the business at home after her day job, and she didn't get paid for that work.

The problem with this scenario is that the business isn't operating on its own. I told the owners that the profit & loss they were producing was fraudulent—it wasn't reflecting the true costs of running a business.

End of story: Pay yourself and any family members working in the business first.

Net Profit Before Taxes (NPBT)

Net profit before taxes is the measurement of success. If sales exceed costs, the profit is positive. If sales are less than costs, the profit is negative.

If a company has a net profit before taxes of $10,000 on $100,000 in sales, they have achieved a 10% net profit before taxes. This could be good or bad, depending on the type of company. In service businesses like heating, ventilation and air conditioning or plumbing, the acceptable profit is 12-20%. Check your own industry association to see the acceptable ranges in your industry.

From that $10,000 noted above, the company must pay all vehicle payments, land payments, loans to banks or shareholders and income taxes. Many costs associated with running a business aren't on the profit & loss and must be noted elsewhere, as described later in this book.

Summary

Remember, the profit & loss is like the speedometer on a car. It shows how fast the business is growing and earning the profits that contribute to net worth. It's bad to go too fast (speeding ticket) and it's bad to go too slow (impeding traffic). You want to use the profit & loss to measure how you're doing each and every month. This isn't a race, but a marathon. If you don't like what your profit & loss reveals, find out why the numbers aren't satisfactory and do something different before next month. We'll talk in detail about the adjustments you can make to become more profitable in later chapters.

CHAPTER 4

MEASURING GROWTH

"A bankruptcy judge can fix your balance sheet,
but can't fix your company."

—*Gordon Bethune*

As we learned in the last chapter, the profit & loss statement shows the profitability of the company. Your profit & loss statement must be reviewed each month so that you have a real-time picture of whether you're making or losing money. If you're losing money, you make immediate adjustments to increase profitability (we'll discuss those adjustments in later chapters). If you're making money, you repeat those same actions month after month and you'll make money for the year.

In this chapter, we'll see how the balance sheet reveals the growth of the company.

Balance Sheet

The balance sheet is like the odometer of the car. It's the history of the company. Just like you'd look at all the repairs and maintenance done over the life of a car to help determine the value of that car, the balance sheet establishes the value of a company. You might think that you could look at the profit & loss statement to determine a company's value, but it's only a window in time. The balance sheet gives the history and it should be reviewed monthly.

The balance sheet is dated with one date, not a range of dates like the profit & loss. The balance sheet shows the company's finances on one day, which will change every day the company is in business.

Let's say you're a heating company and you hang a sign in the cold winter. You'll get business and make money because the current weather will drive your sales. This period of time, the winter, is what the profit & loss would show. It wouldn't show the long-term effects of being in business.

I have provided a sample balance sheet for you to refer to later (see Appendix).

The balance sheet has many layers and categories specific to retail, service or online businesses. All balance sheets are similar, but you may need to track different things for different types of businesses. In this chapter, we'll review the key parts of most balance sheets and why they're important. Then, in Chapter 8, we'll discuss the relationships between the different parts of the balance sheet and what they show about the success of your business.

The balance sheet shows the relationships between three key components of any business:

- Assets (what you own)
- Liabilities (what you owe)
- Net worth (the difference between assets and liabilities)

Exercise

How often does your company produce a balance sheet?

How often do you look at it?

Assets

Assets are things that you've owned from day one.

All assets that you've accumulated that someone might want to buy are in the general asset category. All assets are assigned what they cost, not their value, and are placed into one of three major categories:

- Current assets
- Fixed assets
- Other assets

ASSETS

CURRENT ASSETS
Cash
Accounts Receivable
Employee Receivables
Notes Receivable
Prepaid Expenses
Underbilling (Work in Progress)
Inventory
> **Total Current Assets**

FIXED ASSETS
Building
Office Furniture & Equipment
Machinery & Equipment
Autos & Trucks
Leasehold Improvements
> **Total Depreciable Assets**

Less: Accumulated Depreciation
> Net Book Value

Plus: Land
> **Total Fixed Assets**

OTHER ASSETS

Cash Surrender Value-Officer's Life Insurance
Deposits
> **Total Other Assets**
> **TOTAL ASSETS**

Current assets

Current assets are those assets that the company is going to turn into cash within one year.

Typically, current assets are composed of three main items:

- Cash
- Accounts receivables
- Inventory

These items make up most of the value of the current assets.

Cash is the money that you have in the bank, perhaps your bank balance. It changes every day and includes money to pay bills, suppliers, overhead, salaries, etc.

Accounts receivables is the money owed to you by customers. If you bill customers in a service company, you're issuing invoices which are stored in accounts receivables. Once the customer pays you, the debt is cancelled and the cash is deposited into the cash account.

If the customer doesn't pay you, you can file a lien, take them to small claims court or perhaps issue a 1099c. Check with your tax person for the proper usage of all of these efforts. As a consultant guiding you, a company should have no more than one month's sales in accounts receivables and should have a definitive plan for collection.

Two years ago, a plumber came to my house to repair a leak. I got out my checkbook to pay him, but he said he would just figure the bill and mail it to me. Three months later I called because I still hadn't received the bill. He said he'd get it right in the mail. A month later I called again. He said he'd been too busy to bill anyone but would try. Guess what? He's bankrupt.

If you have a lot of accounts receivables, consider that it may be an internal problem and not a customer problem. All businesses should, where possible, collect before or during the sale—not after. This will increase your cash flow, which we'll discuss at length in Chapter 10. The goal is to get your money, keep it as long as possible to earn interest, and then pay bills at the last minute. If you don't have the customer's money in the bank, you're financing their work with your money.

Inventory are those items that are purchased for resale.

As we learned in the previous chapter when discussing cost of goods sold, many companies sub-divide the inventory items as those that have serial numbers (equipment) and those that don't. Products with serial numbers probably have a warranty from the manufacturer (think: a car or truck). You should record the serial number when the item is purchased and record which serial number is sold to a customer, the new owner.

I've seen thousands of balance sheets and I've learned that many companies don't list inventory at all. They buy inventory, they store inventory in a warehouse or truck and they sell inventory, but they don't have it on the books. Not only is that surprising, it's highly inaccurate.

Remember: When you purchase a part, item or equipment to resell, it goes into inventory. It comes out of inventory when it's sold. That inventory is then removed from the balance sheet and the cost is transferred over to costs of goods sold on the profit & loss statement.

Many companies put all inventory purchases under costs of goods sold. Read that again. It's called cost of goods *sold*, not *bought*. If you do this, you've inflated the costs of each job and lowered your calculated profit.

We discuss inventory control at length in Chapter 11, but these quick tips will get you started:

- Count your inventory as much as you can. I encourage all businesses to count inventory at least every six months. Some retail stores should count at the end of each week. Compare the actual count to the count on the balance sheet and adjust if necessary. Be sure to count the value of the inventory at cost.

- If you're in a service business, clean out all your trucks at least twice a year. Take everything out of the truck. Clean it, replenish it with those items you usually need for jobs and then you'll have a fresh start.

- If you run a service business, don't let technicians stock their own trucks. They will always stock the newest and best item, not the one that is a month old. Why do you think you have all this old inventory that isn't sellable? You need to properly turn your stock.

- Keep track of truck stock. If you stock ten items and sell seven, you should have three in-house. Check, check and re-check.

Inventory is awfully expensive and it's up to you, not others, to control inventory. Controlling inventory can be time consuming and expensive, but it's absolutely necessary. Let me give you a great example:

It isn't unusual to lose 7-15% of your inventory to waste, improper accounting and theft. If you purchase $50,000 of inventory and lose 10%, you've lost $5,000 worth of inventory. Take the $5,000 you lost and divide by your net profit percentage. The value that is calculated is the amount of extra sales necessary to offset the loss. If you lose $5,000 and your profit is 5%, then you need to generate an extra $100,000 in sales to offset the loss. It seems unbelievable, but it's true. How easy is it for you to generate an extra $100,000?

Fixed Assets

Fixed assets are those assets that you use in your business.

Fixed assets are always listed at cost, not value. They're owned by the company and not by you. Buildings, office equipment, cars and trucks are all examples of fixed assets.

Typically these assets lose value over time and we write off their value through depreciation or Section 179 deductions on our tax return. Depreciation reduces the value of the asset over time, generally three to seven years. Section 179 is an immediate write off. It has been around for several decades, but the limit for 2020 is $1,040,000. You can purchase new or used assets that qualify and write off up to $1,040,000 of the cost of the assets, but no more than your net profit. This is a great way to save on your taxes.

Other Assets

These are assets that aren't normally listed in current or fixed but have value.

Examples include goodwill that you purchased, the cash value of a life insurance policy on a key employee and deposits on utilities. You may want to sell these to the buyer of your business, so they do need to be listed.

Exercise

Are all your assets listed on the balance sheet?

What assets do you use in your company that aren't owned by the company?

Who owns them and how is the company compensating the owner for their use?

Liabilities

Liabilities are the short-term and long-term debts of your company.

Liabilities are the bills you owe to suppliers, employees, banks, credit unions and shareholders.

LIABILITIES

CURRENT LIABILITIES
Accounts Payable
Payroll Expenses
Notes and Loans Payable-CurrentPortion
Taxes Payable
Accrued Salaries & Wages
Overbillings or Deposits on Jobs
Reservefor Start-up&Warranty Service
Reserve for Service Contracts or Agreements
Total Current Liabilities

LONG-TERM LIABILITIES

Notes Payable
Less: Current Portion
Total Long-Term Liabilities
TOTAL LIABILITIES

Current Liabilities

Current liabilities are short-term debts and are listed as being paid within one year.

Accounts payable are debts due to suppliers. **Payroll expenses** are debts due to employees and **payroll taxes** are due to state and federal agencies. **Loans** that are going to be paid completely or partially within one year would be placed here as well.

If you happen to sell equipment or a large item and receive a deposit, a category is present that is called **overbilling**. This account means you've accepted money as a **deposit for a job** so you're overbilled. Someone has paid you money, but no work has been done. The deposit isn't a sale, but an overbilling. You put the money in the bank and offset the entry here to show that you're "liable" for at least the deposit money.

A **reserve** is set up for **warranty service**. If you have a warranty on your product or service, how does your company account for the expense? You should set aside, for example, 3–5% of the money you received to pay for warranty work.

Let's say you sell a product for $10,000 that comes with a one-year warranty that you'll honor. Sales should be $9,500 placed on the profit & loss statement and $500 goes into this warranty reserve to cover expenses. After the warranty period has expired, move any money left over into sales.

Many service companies offer a **service contract** or **agreement** to cover parts, materials and equipment maintenance. Typically, this agreement is paid up front and covers a period of time, usually one year. Since the money was collected up front, like a deposit, a sale isn't shown on the profit & loss. You've done no work and had no expenses to offset the money collected. The money you collected stays in this account until you do the work and then the money is moved to the profit & loss statement.

Long-Term Liabilities

Long-term liabilities are defined as those that aren't going to be paid within 12 months.

Examples of long-term liabilities typically include long-term loans for vehicles, property and equipment.

If you bought a vehicle for $40,000 over five years, the first year liability would go under current liabilities. The remainder would go into long-term liabilities. So one-fifth of the $40,000 would go into current liabilities and the remainder, $32,000, would go into long-term liabilities.

One of my clients had given his company over $100,000 of his own money to fund the costs of the business. I asked him where on the balance sheet it showed that he was owed that money. He said he hadn't put any transactions on the balance sheet, so he hadn't shown that the company was paid money and he wasn't shown to be owed money. If no transaction is on the balance sheet, how do you get your money back when money was loaned?

Every time you have a debt associated with the company, it must be recorded on the balance sheet.

Exercise

Into what category would you put a deposit on a job from a customer?

Are lease payments listed on the balance sheet?

Net Worth

Net worth is the difference between assets and liabilities. It can be positive or negative depending on the value of assets and liabilities.

Net worth is the term usually reserved for corporations. The term *proprietorship* is reserved for sole proprietors. The larger the number the better.

NET WORTH
Capital Stock (startup capital)
Paid-In Capital
Retained Earnings (previous years)
Current Earnings (this year)
Total Net Worth

Startup capital is the value of the money and items you used to start the business. If you started your business with $10,000 cash and a $20,000 truck and tools, your startup would be $30,000. **Paid-in capital** is money you paid to the company after startup. **Retained earnings** are profits after tax from previous years that have been retained by the company. **Current earnings** are year-to-date profits after tax for the current year.

This value on your balance sheet shows the value of your company on paper. This isn't a business valuation value, but the value on paper. If you sold all your assets for their value and paid off your liabilities at their value, the money left over is, hopefully, your net worth.

If you make a profit each year, the net worth will increase. If you lose money each year, the net worth will shrink. The goal of any business is to increase their net worth through proper sales, cost control and pricing.

Watch the trend each quarter. Is your net worth growing larger or smaller? If it's growing smaller, locate and remedy the problem.

Your goal as a business owner is to grow your business so that the value increases. Think of your business as a stock. Do you want the stock to go up or down? Do you want the value to be greater or less than cost when you sell?

Summary

In this chapter we discussed the most important document in your company, the balance sheet. The balance sheet shows the wear, tear and growth (or lack thereof) of your company. It's a history of your company and should show if everything you're doing is moving the company in the right direction. You should monitor the balance sheet every month (we'll help with that in Chapter 9) and make corrections monthly. If you find out that you're moving in the wrong direction after one year or before taxes are due, it's too late to make changes, so monitor monthly.

CHAPTER 5:

MAKING YOUR MONEY WORK FOR YOU

"Thinking is the capital, enterprise is the way,
hard work is the solution."

— *A.P.J. Abdul Kalam*

The last chapter focused on the history of the company by examining the balance sheet. Like the odometer on a car, the balance sheet shows the overall history of the company. If you're making the right decisions, you'll make a profit and your net worth on the balance sheet will grow.

This chapter focuses on what to do with the money you make.

Choose Cash or Credit

Do you pay cash for a company vehicle or do you finance it? Which is better? Many companies don't want debt, so they pay cash for everything. Is that the best decision?

When you do make money, you want to think carefully about what you want to do with that money. You need to invest in your business, but also keep enough money for a rainy day. One of my clients made the wrong decision...

My client owned a heating and air conditioning company that had made great money. In fact, the previous year he had made over $200,000 in net profit and had an overall net worth of close to $2,000,000. It was a solid company, they had good personnel and excellent management, but they didn't think about cash.

All of my client's friends were building new buildings, so he got the urge to build a new building too. It seems like he called me every day to complain about not enough room in the office or warehouse—he even complained about the potholes in the parking lot. He could say nothing positive about the business location he had occupied for over 20 years. The new building bug had bitten.

When I went to visit him, he excitedly showed me the plans for the new building and the great financing options. He just knew he could get great rates with only $400,000 down and he couldn't wait to start breaking ground.

Then, Ron the reality coach stepped in. I told him that he couldn't afford to put that much cash into a building because he needed it for cash flow, for a rainy day and to fund other projects. My words flew through him and out the window—he opened his new building eight months later.

Six months after his opening, he wanted to meet me for lunch. When I arrived, I could tell that he was not himself. He confessed that he should have listened to me. He couldn't afford to maintain the building, hire more personnel and keep up with his bills. The extra money he needed, cash flow, was tied up in the new building and he couldn't get it out. In his rush to open a new location, he forgot that you need money to generate money.

If a lot of your money is tied up in assets like buildings and vehicles, you can't use the money to grow the business. Why would you pay $50,000 cash for a new truck, when it's only worth $45,000 when you drive it off the lot? I say, "You have a cash *flaw* in your cash *flow*." You need money to run a company.

Exercise

Should you invest $10,000 in the stock market, real estate or your business? Which one and why?

Understand Working Capital

Working capital is the difference between current assets and current liabilities.

In the previous chapter we learned that current assets are the items that you have in your company that will convert to cash within one year. Current liabilities are items that will be paid off within one year.

The difference between the values, called working capital, is important. This would be the money left over after you cashed in all your current assets and paid off all your current liabilities. Some companies would have nothing left, some would be in the negative and most would be in the positive.

With positive working capital you have money available to take advantage of special hiring situations, rainy days or advantageous pricing. With negative working capital, you can't even pay your bills. Working capital is essential to any business and working capital management is critical.

My banker was visited by a couple who wanted to open a restaurant in a local strip mall. A location was available for only $2,000 per month and it seemed like a great location. They wanted a loan to start the restaurant.

My banker asked the couple how much they had to invest and how much they needed from the bank. They said they had $5,000 and wanted to borrow another $5,000 for a total of $10,000.

The banker then gave them a lesson in working capital management. He said there was no way they could open a restaurant with only $10,000. Rent was $2,000, so they would only have $8,000 left for utilities, furniture, kitchen equipment, supplies, tables, chairs, employees, food, beverages, etc., etc., etc. They would be undercapitalized before they even opened the doors. It takes money to make money.

Exercise

How much cash do you have sitting in the bank?

What percent of sales is the cash you have sitting in the bank?

Is it possible to have too much cash in the bank? Why or why not?

Capitalization—how much working capital you have to run your business—is a major key to success in any business and, depending on the type of business, it can be critical. In small business, the amount of working capital you have and its relationship to profit is interesting. What has been proven is that the amount of working capital has little to no bearing on profitability.

If you have four times the working capital as your competitor, it doesn't mean that you'll be more profitable. If you don't invest the working capital correctly, you may fail. A new concept called working capital turnover helps you decide how much you need to invest in your business to get a proper return on assets.

Working Capital Turnover (WCTO)

Working capital turnover is sales per year divided by working capital.

Let's say your sales are $1,000,000 and your working capital is $100,000. Your working capital turnover is 10. You "turn" your working capital 10 times per year. You go through your working capital about every 36.5 days. You have enough money to pay your bills for 36.5 days with no sales.

Every industry is different, but the chart below shows working capital turnover and its relationship to profit for the contracting industry (heating, ventilation and air conditioning, plumbing and electrical). The vertical axis is profit percentage and the horizontal axis is working capital turnover. The chart shows profitability is at its highest if you have a working capital turnover between 8 and 12. Higher or lower isn't good for the business.

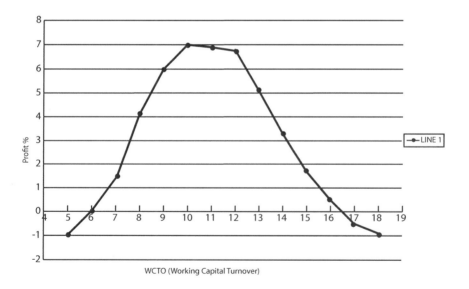

WCTO (Working Capital Turnover)

Let's use our previous example of a business that has $1,000,000 in sales and $100,000 in working capital. The working capital turnover is 10 and falls right in line with the chart. It shows the working capital would be about right to achieve the greatest profit. You don't want to keep your working capital too long, nor do you want to keep it too short. You want just enough to get you through the tough times if sales are slow. That is great working capital management.

Over-Capitalized

If a business has $1,000,000 in sales and $500,000 in working capital, the working capital turnover is 2. This business has 182.5 days of working capital. It doesn't have to sell anything for 182.5 days. They're over-capitalized and that can lead to lazy business practices. Do I even need to open today? Do I even need to answer the phone? As a business, you need to be hungry and motivated to succeed.

Under-Capitalized

If a business has $1,000,000 in sales and $20,000 in working capital, the working capital turnover is 50. The business only has 7.3 days of working capital. This business can only survive 7.3 days without sales. This reminds me of another story I think you'll enjoy...

About 20 years ago I was teaching a financial workshop in Florida, having business owners review their financial documents.

When we got to the calculation for working capital turnover, a business owner in the back of the class asked, "Is 200 too high?"

I asked, "Are you sure you didn't make a mistake?" and immediately went to the back of the room to see what had happened. This business owner's sales were $2,000,000 and his working capital was $10,000. His working capital turnover was correct at 200. He had only about 1.8 days of working capital—he could only survive 1.8 days without selling anything.

Being a good teacher, I told him to stay after class!

This business owner was 27 and looked 57. He was on his phone probably 80% of class time. His fingernails were bitten to the quick and he was one of the most nervous students I had ever encountered. He had been married and divorced twice already.

He said he was a heating, ventilation and air conditioning contractor and was 100% in the new construction market. He got 80% of his business from one builder and the remaining 20% from another builder. He only had two customers providing him with sales and working capital. He was having to spend and collect $10,000 every 1.8 days to survive and keep his business running.

How would you like that pressure?

I gave him several pieces of advice, but most importantly, I told him that the new construction market was too volatile and depended too heavily upon things he could not control. He needed to turn toward the air conditioning replacement business for cash sales to up his working capital.

Just four weeks after my workshop, the builder that gave him 80% of his business announced that he had filed Chapter 11 bankruptcy. When this happened, the owner lost 80% of his working capital. His working capital changed from $10,000 to $2,000 and his working *capital turnover was now 1,000 or 0.3 days.*

Obviously, it became unsustainable for him to continue his business. He actually became a baker.

Summary

As a business owner, you must produce enough sales to not only pay your bills but to have enough left over for working capital. If your working capital turnover is too high, you're overcapitalized and may be hoarding cash and running a lazy business. If your working capital turnover is too low, you're running off credit and barely making ends meet. In a downturn, you risk the loss of your business. You typically want to have enough working capital to cover at least one to three months, but remember that each business is unique and working capital needs may be different.

CHAPTER 6

BREAKING EVEN IS BETTER THAN LOSING

"If you don't know where you're going, any road will get you there."

—Lewis Carroll

n the last chapter we discussed how important working capital is to a business. If you have too much, you risk growing lazy and may ignore the business. If you have too little, you're living paycheck to paycheck and hoping credit will pull you through. You need enough working capital for at least 30 to 90 days in case something happens and you're not able to sell or collect.

This chapter focuses on a concept called breakeven.

Breakeven is the sales dollar volume necessary to pay your bills related to sales.

Think of it as the sales value that generates a zero net profit.

Breakeven would include paying your costs of goods sold (materials, equipment, subcontractors, permits and field labor) and variable and fixed overhead for the period, leaving nothing for profit.

If you were to sell $1,000,000 in products and services to make 10% profit, how much would you need to sell to make nothing? You can even take breakeven down to the month, week, day or hour. I'll show you how to make this calculation and the value it brings to a company.

I once did an evaluation for a plumbing company and found that they needed to sell $400 for every hour they were open just to breakeven. When you know your exact sales goal per hour, you have a very informed goal.

Exercise

How would knowing your breakeven affect your decision making?

Would you like to be able to calculate the breakeven on a salesperson?

How would this knowledge help you?

Breakeven Formula

There are many formulas for breakeven in the small business marketplace, but in my opinion only one is correct. The formula is best applied to a budget (covered in Chapter 16) to see the future or to a past profit & loss to see the past. Look at the budget below and then we'll calculate the breakeven for the company.

BUSINESS BUDGET 2021		
Sales	$1,275,000	100%
Cost of Goods Sold	867,000	68%
Gross Margin	408,000	32%
Variable Overhead	116,600	9.14%
Fixed Overhead	207,350	16.26%
Net Profit	84,050	6.59%

As you can see, the anticipated profit for the company is $84,050 based on sales of $1,275,000. So the question is, how much would the company have to sell to make a profit of $0 or breakeven?

The breakeven formula for small businesses is:

fixed overhead $ / (fixed overhead % + net profit %)

It's important to break your overhead into fixed and variable categories in order to work this formula.

In this example, the fixed overhead is $207,350. The fixed overhead percentage is 16.26 of the sales dollars. The net profit percentage is 6.59.

If we divide the fixed overhead by 22.85%, we get $907,439.82. If they sell $907,439.82 the profit is $0. If they sell over that value, the profit is positive. If they sell under that value, the profit is negative.

If we divide $907,439.82 by 12 months, we see that the breakeven per month is $75,619.98.

Why would a business owner want this number? This number sets the sales goal for the month and it can be used to set quotas for salespeople.

You want to reach this goal as soon as possible during the month be-cause—and this is especially important for this business—for each dollar sold over the breakeven number, 22.85% goes straight to profit. Once you've reached your breakeven point in this example, you have 22.85% profit to play with on making sales.

Another great example of breakeven is calculating the cost of a fixed expense. If you wanted to hire an office person for $40,000 per year, divide $40,000 by 22.85% which tells you how much in additional sales you need to breakeven on the new hire.

Exercise

What is the breakeven value for your company per year?

Per month?

Per day?

What would your breakeven be in hiring a $60,000 salesperson?

How much in sales would they have to do for you to make a profit of zero?

Summary

In this chapter we discussed the concept called breakeven. While you may come across other breakeven formulas, the correct one to use is:

fixed overhead $ / (fixed overhead % + net profit %)

It's important for all businesses to know exactly what sales are necessary to pay the bills associated with sales. This value gives you a baseline for adding fixed assets, personnel and goals for sales compensation.

If you know what your breakeven value is per month, per week and even per day, you'll know before you leave work if you've paid the bills for the day or not.

This value will also help you determine your pricing strategies because you'll know exactly what it costs to sell anything. Just add profit to the breakeven and determine your sale price.

Breakeven is awesome!

CHAPTER 7

GETTING A RETURN ON YOUR INVESTMENT

"So, this is the goal: To make money by increasing net profit, while simultaneously increasing return on investment and simultaneously increasing cash flow."

—Eliyahu Goldratt

I n the last chapter we pointed out the importance of knowing your breakeven so that you can set goals for sales and purchases for the day, month or year. With breakeven, you'll know by the end of each day if you made or lost money. We all want a return for our hard work, right?

That's what this chapter is all about—getting the most from your hard work. When you invest in something, whether it's a business, a home or a boat, you want some kind of return on your money because some day you may want to sell that asset. Properly calculating the return on investment allows you to see if the investment was worth the time and money.

Exercise

Describe the last advertising campaign that you launched.

How much money did it cost you?

Did you measure the results?

How much did it cost you per lead and how much profit did you earn per lead?

What kind of interest rate do you expect at a bank?

Do various investments have different returns?

Return on Investment (ROI)

When you put money into a bank as an investment, you expect a return. The money you put into a savings account at a bank is called *principal*. The money you earn on the savings account is called *interest* and the percentage of interest is called the *interest rate*. If you put $100 into a savings account and get $104 back, you've earned $4.00 interest at an interest rate of 4%.

Do you ever think of your business as a bank? You should. Don't you put money, time and sweat into your business?

In a business the interest earned is called return on investment, or ROI. It's the ratio between net profit and cost of investment.

When you start a business you invest a certain amount of capital to get the business going. Maybe it's a $10,000 truck, $2,000 worth of tools and $1,000 cash. If you total these values, your startup capital would be $13,000. Your job as a business owner is to increase that startup capital and turn it into maximum net worth. You may start with $13,000 but you want to grow that money year after year after year.

My uncle Aus was a great salesman and one of my favorite people. He always took me under his wing and he taught me about hunting, fishing and life. I was already backing his boat into the water when I was eight.

Most of my relatives thought him a bit weird, and he did have some unorthodox ways of doing things, but I loved him. My relatives couldn't understand why he made the decisions he made, but he was very successful.

One day, when I was about eight, my uncle and I were out on his boat. I told him that the family thought he was crazy for buying a Mercedes instead of a Ford or Chevrolet. Why would anyone spend so much money for a car?

He then taught me about return on investment. He said, "I know everyone wants me to drive a Chevy or Ford, but my daddy taught me differently. He told me that a Mercedes was the only car on the market that you could drive for 10 years and then sell for half of what you paid for it. If I bought a Chevy or Ford, it would be worth next to nothing. I think the Mercedes is a better deal."

You're in business to do a better deal. You believe that your $13,000 will grow faster inside your business that it will inside a bank and you're exactly right. Why get 1–2% growth at a bank when you can get 10, 20, 50% or more with the money under your control. Invest in your company and let your hard work be rewarded.

Return on Investment Calculations

The return on investment calculation measures the growth of the company. It measures how much the net worth of the company has increased or decreased. This is the formula for calculating return on investment:

ROI =net profit $ at the end of the sales period / net worth $ at the beginning of the sales period

If a company's net profit was $10,000 at the end of the year and the net worth was $100,000 at the beginning of the year, then the return on investment was 10%. The company earned 10% on their money invested in the company.

You should calculate your return on investment at the end of each month, then at the end of the year. You need to know monthly if your investment is paying off so don't wait until the end of the year to get good financials. If you're making a negative profit, find out why. If you're making a positive profit, find out why.

At the end of the year, if you haven't made a return on investment greater than other investments, why are you still in business? Can you correct the problems?

Return on investment is affected by direct costs, variable overhead, fixed overhead and pricing. If you're not selling—and selling at the right price (Chapter 9)—your return on investment will be low. Check your return on investment frequently.

Return on Investment and Budgeting

Return on investment is also a useful tool in budgeting. When you create a budget, which we cover in Chapter 16, you'll want to use return on investment to project profitability. When most companies do a budget, they project sales first, then costs, then profitability. I advise my clients to start at the bottom with profitability. I always tell clients that it isn't what you sell that keeps you in business, it's profit.

At the beginning of each year, all companies have a total equity, or total net worth, account on their balance sheet. The value in the account shows the value of the business on paper. If you sold all the assets shown on the balance sheet and paid off all the liabilities on the balance sheet, what you have left is total equity, or net worth. This is the money in your "business bank," the money that you want to grow. You want your equity, or net worth, to increase every year.

When you create a budget, you want to project a suitable return on investment for the coming year. For example, if your net worth at the beginning of 2020 was $100,000 and your profit at the end of 2020 was $20,000, your return on investment was 20%. We can use this to project profitability, then sales, then costs.

Take your total equity, or total net worth, value on January 1 and multiply it by a return on investment of 20%, or what your industry statistics show. The value you get will be your projected net profit for December 31.

Then take the profit and divide it by your normal profit & loss profit percentage to get sales.

For example:

Net worth on January 1 = $100,000

Return on investment wanted on December 31 = 20%

$100,000 x 20% $20,000 profit

$20,000 / normal profit percent of 10% = $200,000 in sales

If your calculated sales number is less than your current year sales number, don't use the calculated sales number. Instead use the number of the current year sales times 1.2. I do this because, as a small company, you should be able to grow your sales 20% per year.

Once you have your sales value, work your way down your budget by deducting direct cost percentages, then direct variable overhead percentages and then fixed overhead dollars to determine your true profit percentage.

Summary

Return on investment can be a great tool, not only to see if an expense was worth the cost, but to create a budget. Check your industry through The Risk Management Association (RMA) (rmahq. org) to determine what a reasonable return on investment is for your business. I suggest at least 20% for most businesses, so that will be a great measurement for growth.

CHAPTER 8

EVALUATING YOUR SUCCESS

"That which is measured improves; that which is measured and hangs on the wall improves even more."

—Gerry Faust, Vistage Speaker

I n the last chapter we discussed return on investment, getting the greatest return on our hard work. If we start a business with $10,000 and eventually sell it for $100,000, that's a great return on investment. Every day we must focus on what we need to do to improve our return on investment.

Lewis Carroll wrote the great story Alice in Wonderland. You may remember when Alice, walking through Wonderland, comes to a fork in the road.

Pondering, she says, "I don't know which road to take."

The ever-changing Cheshire cat in the tree asks her, "Where do you want to go?"

Alice replies, "I don't know."

"So," the wise cat says, "If you don't know where you want to go, then it doesn't matter which path you take."

This chapter will show you the path that you need to take to evaluate your success:

- Short-term liquidity and profitability
- Cash flow
- Equity and assets
- Working capital

My son had a sweet Heinz 57-type dog named Tuffy. Every day after dinner we'd let Tuffy out to "visit the neighbors." Tuffy would make his rounds and he always knew exactly where he was going. He ran to the right after leaving the house and returned from the left. He had a destination and he was committed.

One day, about 20 minutes after we let him out, I noticed Tuffy through the glass in the front door. Normally he'd scratch and we'd let him in, but tonight he was just sitting outside.

I opened the door and he quickly ran in. His face was all black and his whiskers were burned, but he had a 16 oz. T-bone with fresh grill marks in his mouth.

He knew the road to take and he took the risk. I just wish we'd had a Go-Pro on his collar to capture a video of that grill owner. That would have been awesome.

Many business owners are a lot more like Alice than they are like Tuffy. They have no short-term goals, no long-term goals and they just stay in business on a day-to-day basis. There's no clear direction and they just want to pay the bills. The problem with this is that they can never stop working because they're too busy surviving. As the owner gets older, the business slows. When the owner retires, the business dies. The owner, the sole proprietor, is the business.

Without goals and measurements, there is no future.

In this chapter, we're going to discuss what to measure and how often. Then I'll introduce you to a program that will make all of these measurements easy and automatic.

Short-Term Ratios

A few monthly measurements are important to see if you're growing, receding or staying the same. We always want to be moving forward, increasing our net worth and our profitability. We need to start by looking at four short-term ratios to determine if we can pay the bills. The information you need for these calculations comes from the profit & loss statement or the balance sheet.

SHORT TERM RATIOS: Liquidity & Profitability			
Current	$\dfrac{\text{Current Assets}}{\text{Current Liabilities}} = \dfrac{1,176,700}{958,900}$	1.1
Quick	$\dfrac{\text{Cash + Accts. Rcv.}}{\text{Current Liabilities}} = \dfrac{604,500}{958,900}$	0.5
Gross Margin	$\dfrac{\text{Gross Profit}}{\text{Sales}} = \dfrac{233,700}{414,100}$	46.3%
Net Margin	$\dfrac{\text{Net Profit Before Tax}}{\text{Sales}} = \dfrac{182,200}{414,100}$	15.5%

Current Ratio

The current ratio is defined as your current assets divided by your current liabilities. Typically your current assets are cash, accounts receivables and inventory. Your current liabilities are your accounts payables, payroll and short-term debt. You divide what you own by what you owe.

For example, if your current ratio is 1.1, then you have $1.10 to pay $1.00 worth of bills. A ratio of 1.5 to 3.0 is a good value in many companies, but you'll want to check your own industry values.

Quick Ratio

This ratio is defined as your cash and accounts receivable divided by your current liabilities. It tells you (or your loan officer) how quickly you can pay the bills. This would also indicate your short-term liquidity.

Looking at the chart above, the quick ratio is 0.5. This company would need to sell something, like inventory, to pay its bills. You always want a value of at least 1.0 for this ratio.

Gross Margin Ratio

This ratio is defined as your gross profit divided by your sales. Gross margin ratio is probably the most confusing ratio in the business world, as the formula can be misrepresented. Gross profit, as we already learned, is defined as sales minus the costs of sales. The confusing issue is costs of sales.

Costs of sales are sometimes called direct costs (see Chapter 11 for more detail) because all costs must be associated with a specific sale or job. If you can causally link the cost to a specific job, the cost is listed under costs of sales. Field labor costs, material costs, supplies costs, inventory costs, permits, cranes, forklift rentals, subcontractors and other costs specific to a job are counted. Sometimes union companies include employee benefits in this category, so be sure you're comparing "apples to apples" in your industry.

Gross margin shows how much of each sales dollar is left over after costs are associated directly with each sale. The higher the margin the better. Gross margin pays for your overhead expenses and gives you profit.

Net Margin Ratio

This ratio is defined as gross margin minus all overhead expenses (see Chapter 11 for more on overhead). Net margin is really called net profit before taxes. This is just the leftover money from sales and their associated expenses. You have to generate enough net profit before taxes to pay other business expenses like bank loans or distributions to stockholders and owners. The more net profit before taxes you generate, the faster your net worth grows and the better your return on investment.

Cash Conversion Cycle Elements

As we learned in Chapter 5, smart companies control their cash and control it well. Simply speaking, it's called managing cash flow. Even though you're selling products and services, your cash may be tied up in assets such as inventory or accounts receivables. If customers don't pay you, you have no money to spend.

Most businesses fail not because of a lack of sales, but because of a lack of cash. You don't have enough cash to pay your bills. Managing cash is essential (see Chapter 10) and there are four formulas that can help you.

CASH CONVERVSION CYCLE ELEMENTS		
Inventory Turn-Days ?	$\dfrac{\text{Inventory X 30 Days}}{\text{COGS (COS)}} = \dfrac{51,300 \times 30}{180,400}$	10
Accounts Receivable Turn-Days ?	$\dfrac{\text{Receivables X 30 Days}}{\text{Sales}} = \dfrac{531,600 \times 30}{414,100}$	50
Average Payment Period-Days ?	$\dfrac{\text{Payables X 30 Days}}{\text{COGS (COS)}} = \dfrac{230,600 \times 30}{180,400}$	40
Cash Conversion Cycle ?	$\text{Inv Days + Rcv Days} - \text{Payment Days} = \dfrac{8.6 + 39.0 -}{38.9}$	20

Inventory Turn-Days

Inventory turn-days indicates the amount of time it takes to "turn" your inventory. In the example listed above, the sample company turns its inventory every 10 days; the inventory only sits on the shelf for 10 days. Money only tied up in inventory for 10 days is good. Imagine holding inventory for a long period of time. Your cash is in inventory and not in your pocket, and the inventory you bought may start becoming unsellable because of its age.

Accounts Receivables Turn-Days

Accounts receivables turn-days shows a business owner how long it takes to collect accounts receivables. This is sometimes called the age of accounts receivables. Obviously, the lower the number the better. You need to collect your accounts receivables as soon as possible to help your cash flow.

Average Payment Period Days

Average payment period days, or aging of accounts payables, shows how long it takes a business to pay its bills. If there is no early payment discount to suppliers or other payables, take as long as you can. You want this number to be greater than your accounts receivables turn-days. You want money to come in from accounts receivables, hold onto it if you can, then pay your bills. Don't spend money until you must.

Cash Conversion Cycles

Cash conversion cycle is the number of days that you must finance your business before money comes in. In our example above, the cash conversion cycle is 20 days. This business must have 20 days' worth of credit or cash available to help it through the cycle before money comes in. A low number, less than 10 days, would be great.

Equity and Asset Ratios

Every business wants a great return on its investment. If you could get a better deal at a bank, why would you waste your time running a business? If your business is returning more than the stock market or a bank, continue on your path to success and keep your money in your business.

RATIOS OF: Equity & Assets*			
Sales to Assets ?	$\dfrac{\text{Sales}}{\text{Total Assets}} =$	$\dfrac{999,900 \times 4}{1,175,967}$	3.0
Return on Assets ?	$\dfrac{\text{Net Profit Before Tax}}{\text{Total Assets}} =$	$\dfrac{269,373 \times 4}{1,175,967}$	46%
Return on Equity ?	$\dfrac{\text{Net Profit Before Tax}}{\text{Equity}} =$	$\dfrac{269,373 \times 4}{191,167}$	261%
Debt to Equity ?	$\dfrac{\text{Total Liabilities}}{\text{Equity}} =$	$\dfrac{984,800}{191,167}$	6.0

Sales to Assets Ratio

Sales to assets ratio shows how well your assets are being used in your company. A large ratio shows that you're doing extremely well. In the above example, assets are generating three times their value in sales. Each industry has their own sales to assets value, and you should compare your number to the industry standard. For example, in the heating, ventilation and air conditioning and plumbing industries, companies should expect a value greater than 5.0.

Return on Assets Ratio

An especially useful formula is return on assets. This tells you how much in sales an asset returns.

Think about the number of trucks in a business that sold $1,000,000 in products and services. Would you want to achieve those sales with one truck? How about with three trucks? Or five trucks?

If you had one truck, you would have produced $1,000,000 per truck. If you had three or five, you would have produced $333,333 or $200,000 per truck respectively.

As you can see, the costs of one truck would be much less than three or five, so the return would be greater. The greater the number on this formula, the better. You want the number to be going up because then you're using your assets even better than the previous month.

Return on Equity (Net Worth)

Return on equity or return on investment (see more in Chapter 7) defines why you're in business. Are you getting the proper return on all the time and effort you devote to the business? Is it really worth it to work all those long hours? Hopefully you're working hard, supporting yourself, your family, your employees and your customers.

Not only do you want a good salary and benefits, but you also want an additional return on your investment of money in the company.

All company data varies, but for a service company such as heating, ventilation and air conditioning or plumbing, you should expect a return greater than 25%. If you're a small company and your equity is small, you may generate a return of 300% or more. Larger companies with large equity, may only generate 15%. The more money you generate inside the company the better.

Debt to Equity Ratio

If you've ever seen your credit score, you've seen a debt to equity ratio. Credit companies measure your debt (how much you owe) and compare it to your equity (how much you own).

If your debt on a $800,000 house is $700,000, you only have $100,000 equity in the home versus the $700,000 debt. Your ratio would be seven to one, throwing a low credit score.

You don't want this ratio to get much above two because then you would be carrying too much debt for the company. However, it's ok to go into debt based on the assets added to equity.

Think about it this way: Is it better to buy a car that has a resell value or to go on an extended vacation using a credit card? The car is the better option because it has residual value verses the debt. The vacation doesn't.

Working Capital Turnover Ratio

We discussed this ratio at length in Chapter 5, but here's another example.

WORKING CAPITAL TURNOVER		
Working Capital Turnover ?	$\dfrac{\text{Annual Sales}}{\text{Average Working Capital}} = \dfrac{3,507,000}{115,250}$	8.5

In the example above, the company has a working capital turnover of 8.5. They "turn" their working capital of $115,250 about 8.5 times during the year. They spend $115,250 and collect $115,250 about every 43 days (365 days / 8.5). They have about 43 days' worth of money to pay the bills. Generally speaking, they can exist about 43 days without selling anything.

Depending upon the industry you're in, you need at least 30 days' worth of working capital—and maybe a lot more if you're billing customers.

Electronic Financial Officer (eFO)

To get you started on your road to financial success, and to give you a roadmap on where you are and where you need to be, eFO will give you the tools to succeed. eFO, developed by FinancialSoft, Inc., was founded by the first-rate team of Bob Carstens and Jack Lance.

With eFO, all the ratios we've discussed in this book are automatically calculated, compared to your industry standards, and then a roadmap to your success is prepared.

This report will show your financial standing in your industry and it will shine a light on what you need to do to grow toward profitability and retirement. It's the first step in the self-evaluation of your company.

You can sign up for a free eFO report by going to collier-consulting. com. Click on the *Products* tab and go to the eFO section. Once you "click here" to access eFO, scroll to the bottom of the eFO page and select *Using QuickBooks Desktop, Using QuickBooks Online* or *Manual Entry (for non-QuickBooks users)* as appropriate.

You can even contact me at ron@collier-consulting.com and I'll walk you through your report. From there you can decide if you want an eFO report monthly to track your successes.

See the summary sample ratio sheet below (part of the full report) and then go to the Appendix to see a full eFO report on a sample company.

Summary

These 13 ratios will tell you and your banker where you are. Are you making or losing money? Is your company growing, dying or existing? If you don't have a reference point, you have no comparison to your industry. Focus on monthly outcomes. Look at your balance sheet, profit & loss statement and eFO report monthly and make changes for the next month if necessary. If you make money each month of the year, you'll probably make money the entire year.

COLLIER CONSULTING GROUP

eFO

Ratio	Formula =	Calculations For Current Month	Actual Annualized	Two (2) Months Ago 7/31/18	Last Month 8/31/18	Current Month + Performance to Goal 9/30/18	Month-to-Month Trend	Goal	Industry Standard Pointer designates current performance verses industry
Report Period Ending 09/30/2018									10% 25% 25% 10% Top Median Bottom
Current	Current Assets / Current Liabilities =	1,176,700 / 959,900	1.1	1.1	1.1	1.2	▲	1.6	1.6 1.5 1.4 1.3 1.3
Quick	Cash + Accts. Rcv. / Current Liabilities =	604,500 / 959,900	0.5	0.5	0.5	0.6	▲	1.2	1.2 1.2 1.1 1.1 1.0
Gross Margin	Gross Profit / Sales =	233,700 / 414,100	46.3%	44.6%	42.1%	56.4%	▲	58.5%	58% 53% 44% 34% 23%
Net Margin	Net Profit Before Tax / Sales =	159,100 / 414,100	6.4%	4.7%	-3.2%	38.4%	▲	7.9%	8.0% 6.5% 2.3% 2.1% 1.8%
Inventory Turn-Days	Inventory X 30 Days / COGS (COS) =	51,300 X 30 / 180,400	10	9	10	9	▼	1	1 2 3 4 14
Accounts Receivable Turn-Days	Receivables X 30 Days / Sales =	531,600 X 30 / 414,100	49	49	55	39	▼	33	33 36 39 44 50
Average Payment Period-Days	Payables X 30 Days / COGS (COS) =	230,600 X 30 / 180,400	39	47	48	39	▼	44	44 37 30 25 19
Cash Conversion Cycle	Inv Days + Rcv Days - Payment Days =	8.6 + 39.0 - 38.9	20	11	17	9	▼	-10	-10 1 12 23 45
Sales to Assets	Sales / Total Assets =	999,900 X 4 / 1,175,967	3.0	2.9	2.9	3.4	▲	5.2	5.2 5.1 4.8 4.5 3.2
Return on Assets	Net Profit Before Tax / Total Assets =	166,100 X 4 / 1,175,967	19%	12.1%	-2.4%	56.5%	▲	14.0%	14% 12% 11% 10% 6%
Return on Equity	Net Profit Before Tax / Equity =	166,100 X 4 / 191,167	108%	88.6%	-18.5%	347.6%	▲	58.9%	50% 51% 48% 39% 11%
Debt to Equity	Total Liabilities / Equity =	984,800 / 191,167	6.3	6.3	6.6	5.2	▼	1.2	1.2 2.5 3.0 3.8 4.4
Working Capital Turnover	Annual Sales / Average Working Capital =	3,507,000 / 216,800	22.7	36.4	35.7	22.7	▼	8.0	8 10 15 20 30

More Information

Goal Setting Tutorial

CHAPTER 9

PRICING FOR PROFIT

"The difference between a corrupt and an honest person; the corrupt person has a PRICE and the honest person has VALUE."

—Unknown

This is my favorite chapter. Most business owners start a business by not understanding pricing and go bankrupt by not understanding pricing. I want to change that.

I asked one of my clients, the owner of a heating, ventilation and air conditioning contracting company, how he set his hourly service call rates when he started his business.

He said he called two other contractors in his market. One charged $60 per hour and one charged $80 per hour, so he set his hourly rate at $70 per hour. He didn't want to be too high, but he wanted to be in the ballpark.

Another client quit a heating, ventilation and air conditioning com-

pany and started his own company. The problem was that he had no customers, just a truck and some tools. He found that the lowest rate in town was $40 per hour and the highest was $80 per hour (at the company where he was previously employed).

Since he had no work, his thought process was to set his hourly rate at $40 per hour to pull customers from his old employer.

That's like quitting a Mercedes dealership and opening a Kia dealership, hoping that a Mercedes customer will buy a Kia.

When you set your hourly rate at $40 per hour, you get $40 per hour customers—customers whose perceived value for one hour of service is $40. This is the question for all companies: Do you want to be the cheapest in town, the highest in town or somewhere in between? We'll answer this question shortly.

Exercise

Are there any advantages to being the lowest price in town?

Are there any advantages to being the highest price in town?

What do you think your customers want—price, service or quality?

Volume and Price-Sensitive Businesses

All businesses make money through either volume selling or price selling.

Volume-Sensitive Businesses

Volume sensitive businesses have a fixed overhead expense greater than 50% of sales. It costs them a tremendous amount just to open the doors.

Think about big box stores and their payroll, utilities, benefits and inventory. They must sell a large volume of products every day to pay for their overhead. Because this is true, they can also manipulate price daily. If they normally sell tomatoes for $1.00 per pound, they can sell some for $0.50 per pound because they sell 1,000 per day. Their price can change anytime, even daily, to encourage buying because they have the volume to make up for it.

Think about an airline. Their costs to fly from point A to point B is about the same regardless of the number of passengers. Their fixed costs are high. Initially they want to fill the plane with passengers, so they offer low fares. As the plane starts filling up, the prices start going up. If everyone wants to go to Las Vegas, the first passengers probably pay the lowest fare and the last passengers probably pay the highest. Airlines never want to fly a plane with an empty seat.

The point I am making is this: If your business sells 1,000 items per day and has a fixed overhead greater than 50% of sales, you're volume sensitive. You need volume to make money, so you can have many pricing strategies to achieve your profit goal.

Price-Sensitive Businesses

Most businesses, especially mom and pop shops, aren't volume sensitive, they're price sensitive.

Price sensitive businesses have a low fixed overhead expense and need proper pricing to make money. Since these businesses don't sell in volume, they need to protect price and can only offer minor discounts. They can't make up pricing mistakes with volume. Pricing should be set and discounts should be rare and extremely limited. Most all small businesses fall into this category.

Several years ago I helped one of my heating, ventilation and air conditioning clients create a budget. We created a budget with sales of $800,000 and a net profit of $40,000, or 5% of sales.

At the end of our discussion, my client said that he worked too hard to earn a profit of just $40,000 and I agreed. He wanted $25,000 more.

I told him that in any business there were only three ways to make money: increase sales revenue, cut costs of doing business or raise price.

Which is the best choice for my client: increasing sales revenue, cutting costs or raising prices?

There's a financial formula you can easily use with your business to answer that question.

sales $ = net profit $ / net profit %

We'll use my client as an example. To make $25,000 more on the bottom line through increased sales revenue, the formula becomes sales $ = $65,000 / 5%. The calculation reveals that sales needs to be $1,300,000. This client needs to increase his sales $500,000, or 62.5%, to reach his profit goal of $65,000.

To make $25,000 more on the bottom line through reducing costs of doing business, we decided that a cost reduction of 3% was possible. The formula became sales $ = $65,000 / 5% + 3%. The cost savings becomes profit. So the calculation becomes $65,000 / 8% = $812,500. If he dropped 3% of costs from his business, he wouldn't have to sell $800,000, but $12,500 more to reach his profit goal of $65,000.

To make $25,000 more on the bottom line through a price increase, the formula becomes profit % = extra profit $ / sales $. It's the same formula, but we just moved it around. The profit he wants is an additional $25,000 / sales of $800,000 = 3.125%. He would need to increase the price of all his products and services 3.125% to achieve his profit goal of $65,000.

My client has three choices:

- Increase sales 62.5%
- Cut costs 3%
- Raise prices 3.125%

They each have the same effect on the bottom line of his business.

Do you think it's easier to increase sales 62.5% or to raise prices 3.125%?

Can you see why this company is price sensitive? A small price increase has a huge impact on the bottom line, and it's easy to do.

My workshop attendees love this discussion because they'd normally raise prices as a last resort, not a first resort. Most attendees want to increase sales first without even knowing if they're priced correctly.

Now for the bad news: this also works in reverse. If this client dropped his price 3.125% for one customer, he would have to sell to 1.625 customers at regular price to make up for the discount. Price-sensitive businesses must be incredibly careful when they offer discounts, and any discounts must be rare and short-lived.

Pricing Strategies

Pricing strategies are one of, if not the most, important issues in any business. How you set your price determines how you present your company to the type of customers you want to attract.

A person I met wanted to sell bottled rainwater as drinking water. Tremendous concept as it's pure water, but he had a problem with pricing. When we spoke over dinner, he said he could produce a pint of rainwater including the bottle, water and label for about 37 cents. He wanted to sell it for 69 cents. His gross margin would be 32 cents for each bottle sold to cover his overhead and give him a profit.

I told him to finish his dinner so we could leave.

I took him to the convenience store and asked him to find a 69 cent bottle of water. He couldn't. I then asked him to find the least expensive water and the most expensive water. He came back and said that the least expensive was 99 cents and the most expensive was $1.49. I then explained the 2 parts of pricing to him: profit and market.

Yes, he could make money selling his water for 69 cents, but the market range had already been established between 99 cents and $1.49. He was also selling rainwater—not spring water or distilled water. He should position himself at the upper end of the range and sell at about $1.29.

The points to be made are these:

- You need to set your price initially to:
    - Cover your costs of goods sold
    - Cover your variable overhead
    - Cover your fixed overhead
    - Give you a great profit for your efforts

- Then, you need to see what the market will bear and adjust your price accordingly.

If my client had to sell his water at $2.00 per bottle to make any money, he would have had trouble because the market would say he was too high.

Strategic Market Pricing

Let's consider the products and services you're offering right now. Create a line like the one shown below:

Let's say you perform service work and you charge per hour. You investigate your market and determine the lowest and highest charges per hour. For example, in your market the lowest price per hour is $60 and the highest is $120. Your line would look like this:

Take your lowest number, $60 in this case, and subtract it from your highest number, $120. The value you get, $60 in this example, is the difference. Divide the difference by 4 to get what we call the spread. The spread is the distance between the letters D, C, B and A. In this case, the spread is $15, so the line should look like this:

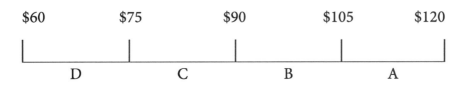

This line represents the market that you serve, and we've divided it into quadrants. Finally, put an X on the line at the rate you charge. In the example below, the client charges $70 per hour.

| $60 | $75 | $90 | $105 | $120 |

D   C   B   A

So why am I taking you through all this drawing and math? To show you where you are in your market. You're either a D, C, B or A business.

Why is this client charging $70 per hour when the most expensive place charges $120? Is his competitor worth $50 more per hour? His customers think so.

Research in the heating, ventilation and air conditioning and plumbing industries showed something very remarkable. The companies that made double digit profits were priced in the upper 35% of their market. Their X would have been from the midpoint of B through A.

In this example, if the costs of service are $50 per hour and the company charges $70 per hour, then the profit is $20 per hour. When they bill 100 hours, they make $2,000.

If they were to raise their rate to $80 per hour, their costs wouldn't change but their profit would now be $30 per hour. They would only need to bill 67 hours to make the same money. One third less time, one third less costs, one third less people and one third less trucks to make the same money. If you're too busy, your price is too low.

To make the most money, and to be a value-added business, your pricing should be in the upper 35% of the market in service and in the upper 50% of the market in retail. Now I'll show you how to calculate your price and determine if it's in the correct range.

Strategic Pricing Strategies

When I first joined the contracting business back in the 1980s, I always wondered how business owners priced their jobs or their product. So I just asked them.

One business owner told me how he calculated what to charge a homeowner to install a new air conditioning and heating system in a home.

He would enter the home and count the number of doorknobs inside the home. Bedrooms, bathrooms, closets—all doorknobs were counted. He then multiplied the number of doorknobs by $400 and that was his price for the job.

After this explanation, he asked me for advice on why he was losing money.

Another business owner said that he counted the legs in the house. The more legs in the house, the more air conditioning and heating they needed. Humans counted as two legs each and pets, since they were small, counted as one leg. So, a couple with a dog would total five legs. He multiplied the legs by $600 and priced the job. He even used the same method to size the house for the correct heating and air conditioning system. He took the legs and divided by two and that was the size system that the *thought the house needed in tons of cooling. Simple, easy—and totally inaccurate. He eventually went bankrupt.*

It's hard to believe these stories, but many companies start their business before they ever think about pricing. They don't know their true costs of doing business and they don't price before they open. Even then, most companies price way too low. While they get business at those prices, they're just paying the bills and never getting ahead.

I've examined many pricing strategies throughout the years and I've found the two most accurate:

- The gross margin method should be used for retail businesses because they primarily sell inventory.

- The dual overhead allocation method should be used for service and installation businesses because they sell labor and inventory.

Let's take a look at both.

Gross Margin Method

For most all retail businesses that receive their revenue from selling inventory (like a jewelry store), the gross margin method is the most useful. Remember, gross margin is the % of sales dollars leftover to pay for overhead and profit.

The formula is:

sale price = estimated costs of the sale / (100% - gross margin % wanted)

If you buy an inventory item for $1.00 and need 75% gross margin to cover overhead and profit, the formula becomes sale price = $1.00 / (100% - 75%) or $1.00 / 25%. The sale price would be $4.00.

We use this formula in retail because you normally don't charge a customer for labor if you're selling inventory. You're only charging them for the inventory item that you're selling—the sale of the inventory item covers the labor cost.

Gross margin will cover your labor because it's in overhead and not in costs of sales. Grocers have a margin of about 20 to 28% while other retail stores may average 50% or higher.

Dual Overhead Allocation Method

The best method for companies that sell both labor and inventory is dual overhead. This method has been used for over 40 years, primarily in the new construction market, but it has worked its way into the retail and service industry.

If you sell both labor and inventory, you are considered a service business. When service businesses quote jobs, they must determine the cost of labor and the inventory they're going to use on the job.

Labor includes field labor only, not salaried positions.

Inventory includes what we'll call MESO, which is made up of costs of materials, equipment, subcontractors and other costs like permits and rentals.

Since service companies sell both labor and inventory, they also need to consider how much overhead must be assigned to the job.

Think about pricing for a moment. If a field person costs you $30 per hour, you may "sell" that person for $100 per hour. The $100 covers the $30 for the person plus $70 for overhead plus profit. Most companies don't know how the $70 is divided, so they don't know how much is overhead and how much is profit. Most companies also don't know if the $100 actually covers everything.

If you buy a part for $10 and sell it for $30, how much of the $20 that you have left goes to overhead and profit? Again, most companies don't know the answer.

Many years ago I asked one of my clients how he priced his jobs when he started his company. He said that he took the actual costs of the job and multiplied that times three: one for the costs of the job, one for the overhead on the job and one for profit. He was successful, but he was guessing.

Dual overhead is extremely accurate and I've been using the formula with my clients for decades. Not only will it price all jobs correctly, you can use the formula to calculate overhead distribution to profit centers. All service companies should use this formula, but let me first set the ground rules.

This formula should be calculated for your business twice per year. I suggest February (after you've completed the previous year's financials and the new year's budget) and September (before the last quarter). Using your year-to-date financials, you'll tweak the formula, updating it to your current financial situation.

Let's get started…

The dual overhead formula looks at your profit & loss statement and analyzes how much you spend for field labor in relation to how much you spend on MESO. Using this information, it calculates how much overhead should be allocated to the job for field labor and MESO. Adding the allocated overhead to the job gives you the breakeven for the job, then you add the profit you want.

I want to stress that dual overhead is the best method for service companies because it gives you the number all business owners need—breakeven for the job. If you know exactly how much a job is going to cost you before you present your bid or proposal, your accuracy in profit forecasting and job costing goes up exponentially. Don't stop reading now!

Dual overhead has three formulas:

Formula 1:   *MESO to labor ratio = (costs of materials + equipment + subcontractors + other) / (costs of field labor)*

Formula 2:   *overhead rate on labor = (X) (overhead) / [(X) (Field Labor) + (MESO)]*

Formula 3:   *overhead rate on MESO = overhead rate on labor / (X)*

These values come from your profit & loss statement. I suggest that you use this year's profit & loss statement if it has data for at least nine months. If it doesn't, use last year's profit & loss statement.

Let me guide you through an example to show you how it's done. The following is the data we'll use off a profit & loss statement:

MESO $233,450
Field Labor $147,150
Overhead $184,570

Formula 1:   MESO to labor ratio
                      $233,450 / $147,150 = $1.59

Formula 2:   Overhead rate on labor (use the chart below to get the X value and interpolate if needed)

                      (X) (overhead) / [(X) (field labor)] + MESO =

                      (2.86) ($184,570) / [(2.86) ($147,150)] + ($233,450) = 0.81

Formula 3:   Overhead rate on MESO
                      Rate on field labor / X
                      0.81/2.86 = 0.28

Ok, catch your breath! Still with me? Let me explain further.

Formula 2 shows an overhead rate on field labor of 0.81. This means that for every dollar you spend on field labor you "spend" 81 cents for overhead. You must allocate $0.81 for every $1.00 it costs you for field labor. If it costs you $30 per hour in wages for a field person, you must add (0.81) x ($30) or $24.30 for overhead. Your breakeven on the $30 wage is $30 + $24.30 or $54.30 per hour. See how great this is?!?

Formula 3 shows the overhead rate on MESO of 0.28. For every dollar you spend on materials, equipment, subcontractors and other costs, you also "spend" 28 cents for overhead. You must allocate $0.28 for every $1.00 it costs you for MESO. If you buy a part for $100, you must add $28 for overhead allocation. Your breakeven for the part is $128.

Using these values, let's price a job based on the following costs:

Costs	Overhead	Breakeven
Materials	$400 + (0.28) ($400)	$512
Equipment	$180 + (0.28) ($1800)	$2,304
Subcontractors	$200 + (0.28) ($200)	$256
Other	$100 + (0.28) ($100)	$128
Field Labor	$400 + (0.81) ($400)	$724
TOTAL	$2,900 + $1,024	$3,924

The breakeven value of $3,924 covers all costs and overhead related to the job, but zero profit. That's why this number is called breakeven. If you want to get the job, you need to add in profit. Thus, another formula is needed.

selling price = breakeven for the job / 100% - net profit % wanted

For example, if you wanted a 20% profit on this job, the formula would be:

selling price = $3,924 / 100% - 20% = $3,924 / 80% = $4,905

In conclusion, the dual overhead method is the best method if you have a service company and sell both inventory and labor. Since each job will be different, overhead will change on every job. If a job is labor intensive, the overhead allocation will be higher. If a job is MESO intensive, the overhead allocation will be smaller.

What's important in dual overhead is breakeven, which can't be calculated with other pricing strategies. Then you can change the profit to meet the merits of the job. Regardless, breakeven doesn't change, only the profit.

For more information, visit my website collier-consulting.com. For software that will quickly calculate dual overhead numbers, visit profittrackersoftware.com.

Dual Overhead X Values

(1) MESO/L	(2) X	(3) MESO/L	(4) X	(5) MESO/L	(6) X	(7) MESO/L	(8) X	(9) MESO/L	(10) X
0.0	1.82	3.8	4.30	7.6	6.20	11.4	7.26	15.2	7.76
0.1	1.88	3.9	4.36	7.7	6.24	11.5	7.28	15.3	7.77
0.2	1.95	4.0	4.42	7.8	6.28	11.6	7.30	15.4	7.78
0.3	2.01	4.1	4.48	7.9	6.31	11.7	7.31	15.5	7.79
0.4	2.07	4.2	4.54	8.0	6.35	11.8	7.33	15.6	7.80
0.5	2.13	4.3	4.60	8.1	6.38	11.9	7.35	15.7	7.81
0.6.	2.20	4.4	4.66	8.2	6.42	12.0	7.37	15.8	7.81
0.7	2.26	4.5	4.71	8.3	6.45	12.1	7.38	15.9	7.82
0.8	2.33	4.6	4.77	8.4	6.49	12.2	7.40	16.0	7.83
0.9	2.39	4.7	4.82	8.5	6.52	12.3	7.42	16.1	7.84
1.0	2.46	4.8	4.88	8.6	6.55	12.4	7.43	16.2	7.84
1.1	2.53	4.9	4.94	8.7	6.59	12.5	7.45	16.3	7.85
1.2	2.59	5.0	5.00	8.8	6.62	12.6	7.46	16.4	7.86
1.3	2.66	5.1	5.05	8.9	6.65	12.7	7.48	16.5	7.86
1.4	2.72	5.2	5.10	9.0	6.68	12.8	7.49	16.6	7.87
1.5	2.79	5.3	5.16	9.1	6.71	12.9	7.51	16.7	7.88
1.6	2.86	5.4	5.21	9.2	6.74	13.0	7.52	16.8	7.88
1.7	2.93	5.5	5.26	9.3	6.76	13.1	7.53	16.9	7.89
1.8	2.99	5.6	5.31	9.4	6.79	13.2	7.55	17.0	7.89
1.9	3.06	5.7	5.36	9.5	6.82	13.3	7.56	17.1	7.90
2.0	3.13	5.8	5.41	9.6	6.85	13.4	7.57	17.2	7.91
2.1	3.19	5.9	5.46	9.7	6.87	13.5	7.59	17.3	7.91

Flat Rate Pricing for Service and Installation Companies

Right after World War II, service businesses, including car repair specialists, began to offer flat rate pricing once a job was estimated. Consumers no longer wanted to pay per hour or per piece. Service businesses began to quote flat, not changeable, prices for their work and soon it became acceptable everywhere—even at restaurants, cafeterias and repair specialists.

Once the problem is determined, the business quotes a flat fee that includes all parts and labor for the job. Time was removed from the discussion and all labor was standardized. Part of the fee was labor regardless of who did the work and how long it took. Part of the fee was parts regardless of how many were used.

Today, flat rate is the best presentation method and the most accepted by consumers. Most companies that use flat rate pricing make 20 to 25% more per job. That really gets the profit you deserve!

Oil change centers who charge $39.95 exhibit this type of pricing strategy the best. No time is priced and no filter or oil is itemized. Regardless of the time or materials used, the price is the same for all customers. Oil change centers teach us something else: never round a sales price.

Most companies print their own flat rate books or use a pricing file on their tablet or online. Each person in the field—and at least one person in the office—needs a flat rate book to quote a price to a customer. In addition to the price for the service or repair, a service call fee is added to offset travel and cover diagnosis of the problem.

Service companies today charge about six to seven times the wage rate for their labor and then markup their parts from around 6.5 to 1.33 using a variable markup table like the one below. Multipliers to determine sale pricing change about every $3 to $5 change in costs.

Cost of Part Multiplier

$0–2.99	6.5
$3–5.99	6.375
$6–8.99	6.25
$9–11.99	6.125
$12–14.99	6.00
Etc.	0.125 increments

For more information about flat rate pricing in the contracting industry, visit collierflatrate.com and download a sample parts multiplier table that can be used by any type of business.

Summary

In this chapter we discussed various pricing methods and the ones that work best. So many price-sensitive companies go out of business during the first three years because they try to price like volume companies. The owners work too many hours to achieve the volume they need to be successful, and finally they just give up and close.

Whether you're a contracting company (a company that does mainly installations) or service company (a company that usually does more service than installations), remember that customers want to know what it costs overall, not how much you charge per hour. They prefer the optics of flat rate pricing, so switch to this method and charge per job.

CHAPTER 10

COLLECTING YOUR PROFITS

"It's not how much money you make, but how much money you keep, how hard it works for you, and how many generations you keep it for."

—*Robert T. Kiyosaki*

In the last chapter we discussed how to price properly. Pricing is probably the number one key to profitability and should never be taken lightly. If your products are priced so that you can make money and the price is favorable with the market, you'll have a solid business—if you can keep the money you earn.

Cash flow is the money that moves in and out of the bank. You can sell an item today, but the money may not hit your bank account until weeks later. You could have a great sale but could still be broke. That's what cash flow is all about.

Unfortunately, I've seen many businesses fail because of a lack of cash, not because of a lack of sales or customers. No matter what you sell, if your collection strategies aren't consistent, you can easily fail.

This chapter focuses on collection strategies so that you can keep the money that you earn. Sell at a profit and get your money quickly so that you can pay your bills. As someone once said, "Collect early and pay late." The longer you hold money, the more your company will prosper.

Exercise

Have you ever experienced a cash flow problem?

If so, what caused the problem?

What did you do to correct the problem?

Years ago, a colleague and I went to a company that was having a lot of problems and couldn't keep up with their bills. Their accounts payables kept stacking up and they were about $12,000 behind in payments.

In visiting with the owner, he told me that he didn't know what the problem was as they were busy and his pricing was correct. He was selling a lot and his marketing was working, but he was frustrated with the cash flow.

About an hour later, I met with his office manager. Her office was very

*disorganized, with papers everywhere, even on the floor. She was in-
credibly nervous about our visit and smoked profusely (this was back
in the day when smoking indoors was a thing). She kept rolling her
chair across the floor, crushing papers on the floor as we spoke.*

*I asked her, "Are those papers that you're rolling over important?" She
replied, "Yeah, somewhat, but they're just checks."*

*I couldn't believe what she had just said. I asked again, "What did you
say was on the floor?"*

She replied "Checks."

*Her accounting practices were clear: she was holding all the checks that
had come in until all the paperwork from all the invoices was properly
completed and all the jobs were job costed. Some of the bills, paperwork from the field or even invoices from supplies and materials on
jobs didn't come in for several weeks. She didn't deposit the check for
the job until everything was in. Some checks were over four months
old! As we began to get the checks off the floor and total them, there
was over $27,000 available.*

I always say that you can tell when a company has cash flow problems. They exhibit one of these three behaviors:

1. They check the mailbox every day.
2. They meet the mail person who is bringing the mail at the door.
3. They wait for the post office to open.

Many companies sell too much and forget to collect. On average, according to government statistics, an accounts receivable loses about 8% of its value every 30 days. So if you bill and don't collect, the value of what you bill diminishes every day.

Cash Flow

As we learned earlier, cash flow is needed to pay bills and sustain growth. You need cash flow immediately, even if you're going to start a business.

Imagine going to a bank to get a loan to open a new salon. You've found a great location with a great rental price, but now you just need the money to actually open the business. You show the banker your plan and then ask him for the money.

He asks, "How much do you need?"

You reply, "I need $10,000 to open my salon."

He would probably say that you've failed prior to opening. You don't have enough cash to be successful. Don't you need to furnish the rental, buy and install equipment, hire employees and pay for advertising? You don't have enough cash flow for the business to be successful. You'd run out of cash before the first sale. Bankers know this and so should you.

Similarly, a friend of mine paid cash for a $40,000 car, then couldn't afford the insurance and gas. Cash is king, so be sure you have enough to meet your obligations.

How can you tell if you have enough money to pay the bills? You have to look at your profit & loss statement and you bank statements. The profit & loss tells you how much you sold and the costs of those sales, but that's different from the bank statement. The bank statement tells you what you deposit (not what you sold) and the bills you paid (not what the costs were to sell). You need both in a timely manner to determine cash flow.

Here's an example of what happens in a normal workflow:

You sell a product for $2,000 and the customer asks to be invoiced. You go to your supplier and pick up a $1,000 product and the supplier bills your account.

How much money did you deposit into your bank account from the sale? Zero.

How much money did it cost you for the product today? Zero.

Your profit & loss shows a sale of $2,000 and a cost of $1,000, but no money was credited or debited. Your cash flow didn't change because your bank account didn't change. You realized a $1,000 profit, but that profit wasn't deposited.

Exercise

Do you have a plan for accounts receivables collections?

Do you charge customers interest on their overdue accounts or a billing charge?

How long does it take for your office to bill a customer?

How often do you review an aging report?

Accounts Receivables Aging

As we've already established, it's important to produce a balance sheet, profit & loss statement and cash flow statement every month. Look carefully at the profit & loss to show sales, costs and profit activity, but keep in mind that the sales revenue dollars and checks for costs may not have made it to your bank. They may be delayed. It's the cash flow statement that reveals these inconsistencies.

All sales have aging revenue.

Current aging is the money you collect at the time of sale.

Most retail establishments have current aging.

Aging is the money you collect after the sale.

Most service and contracting companies have aging. They bill the customer and don't get the money for 30, 45 or even 60 days.

The longer you wait to receive payments, the more difficult it will become to pay your bills and your employees.

Be sure to look at the jobs you take before you sign a contract. A large sale may look great until you review the payment terms. Many contracts hold a retainer of 10% for months until the whole job is completed—and that 10% might be your entire profit. Do you have enough money to fund the job through months of billing and retainage?

The following charts show the cash flow of one of my clients (name changed for privacy). Nothing else changed in the business, but look at the changes as they moved from current billing to 30 days to 45 days to 60 days.

Current Aging of Accounts Receivables

By collecting on the spot and not invoicing, the cash flow for this company is excellent. They have plenty of money to pay their bills every month of the year.

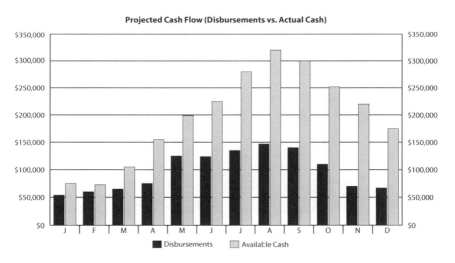

Projected Cash Flow (Disbursements vs. Actual Cash)

Disbursements ■ Available Cash □

30-day Aging of Accounts Receivables

The company adopted an invoicing policy of billing customers and not receiving payments for 30 days. Cash flow is ok and they can meet each month's obligations, but notice the amount of cash they have each month compared to the current billing chart above.

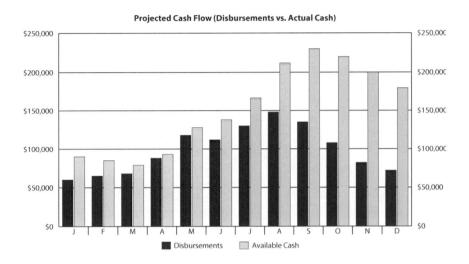

45-day Aging of Accounts Receivables

The company chose to collect sales revenue every 45 days and you can see the effect. Now they're experiencing cash flow problems four months of the year and they don't have enough money to meet their cost obligations.

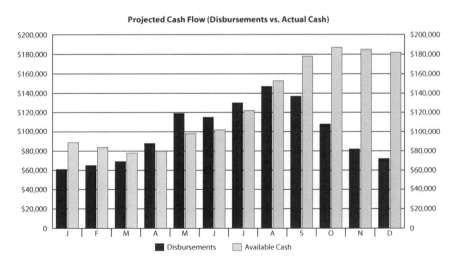

60-day Aging of Accounts Receivables

The company chose to collect receivables every 60 days and look at the impact to cash flow. Now they're experiencing cash flow problems with large gaps six months of the year.

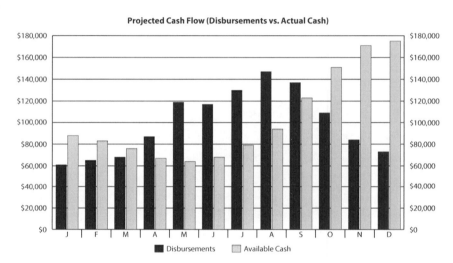

Projected Cash Flow (Disbursements vs. Actual Cash)

■ Disbursements ☐ Available Cash

What you've seen above is only a change in accounts receivables. It's important to bill as quickly as possible and to pay your bills as late as possible, keeping cash close to the business. Follow these guidelines:

- Don't pay bills late if there is a late fee, but do pay bills early if there's a discount. A 1% / net 10 discount equals about an 18% APR. If you can borrow money at less than 18% APR, borrow the money and take the discount.

- Develop a specific, written collections policy.

- Issue all invoices to customers net due upon receipt.

- Don't send statements to customers. A statement is not an obligation for payment. Send an initial invoice, then another past due invoice if needed. You may even want to call them if you haven't received your money within 10 days of invoicing.

- Many companies get into cash flow problems because of internal decisions. If customers don't pay you, look internally first to see if proper collection procedures are being followed.

I received a phone call from a heating, ventilation and air conditioning dealer one August. I asked him how his sales were going. He replied that his business had been so good, and he had been so busy, that he had not had the chance to bill his customers for the last three months.

Summary

It's important to produce both monthly profit & loss statements and balance sheets, but it's also just as important to produce a cash flow statement. Sales don't equal deposits, so you want to be sure that you know how much money you have available to spend. Also, if you bill, be sure to look at an aging report of your accounts receivables so you know who has—and has not—paid you. Cash is king in any business and you need to be sure you have enough. As we discovered in Chapter 5, too much cash is bad and so is too little.

CHAPTER 11

CONTROLLING COSTS

"When you're in business for a long time, you go through good times and bad times. When you go through bad times, you learn to control costs, satisfy customers better, satisfy employees better and become more transparent. Therefore, you build character in the company."

—N.R. Narayana Murthy

In the last chapter, we discussed cash flow and its impacts on the business. As I previously noted, most businesses fail not from a lack of sales, but from a lack of cash. When we collect cash, we want to keep more of it to use in the business.

Controlling costs can help. As we've already learned, there are only three ways to make money in any business: increase sales, cut costs or raise price. Raising price is the most direct approach to increasing profit because it can be done immediately. Cutting costs is also effective and while it requires time to evaluate and implement, many costs can be reduced or eliminated.

As part of this process, I recommend that your business bank statements be delivered to your home so that you can review them and look at all checks written. Do you see any unknown vendors or anomalies? Then take the bank statement to the office for reconciliation.

Types of Costs

In any business there are three types of costs:

- Direct (also known as job costs)
- Indirect variable overhead
- Indirect fixed overhead

To properly analyze your business, your accounting software should account for these categories and should reflect not only what you spend in dollars but also as a percent of sales. These values can help you evaluate whether you're spending too much or too little, as compared to industry standards.

Direct (Job) Costs

Direct costs include those costs that could be directly billed to a customer (preferably as part of flat rate pricing, not broken out as line items). These costs don't exist if there is no customer. Typical direct costs include direct labor, direct materials or supplies, direct equipment, direct warranty or extended warranty and other (miscellaneous costs) like a permit for a job. If you can specifically tie the cost to a job, then it's a direct, billable cost. Direct costs don't include inventory purchased, only inventory purchased and sold.

Indirect Variable Overhead

These are the costs that accumulate with sales. They typically go up as sales go up and down if sales go down. Credit card charges are examples, because the more you sell, the more credit card charges you'll accumulate. Gasoline and auto repairs are other examples.

Indirect Fixed Overhead

Indirect fixed overhead costs are those costs that typically stay the same regardless of sales. Rent, salaries and utilities would be found in this category.

When sales revenue changes, direct and variable overhead costs also change, but fixed costs remain the same.

Exercise

Which costs do you find the most difficult to control?

Why?

I once visited a contractor who was having financial trouble. Her company's net profit was negative so she invited me in to help assess the damage.

Her pricing was all over the place and her costs were too high. She had just spent over $6,000 to install video cameras in her inventory room and parking lot. She couldn't pay her bills but spent $6,000 on a video camera. She had no specific knowledge of inventory theft, but she wanted to stay current with technology.

I told her this was a poor decision; she really needed to control her costs. I gave her a list of items that were too high, including phone bills, gasoline and advertising, but she refused my suggestions.

She seemed to only want more sales so that she could buy what she wanted. She refused to grow her company for profit.

Controlling Direct Costs

Let's take a critical look at the costs of doing business.

Suppliers

Keep enough inventory and supplies in your truck and/or office to take care of your customers for at least one week. Find a dependable supplier and have them stock for you on consignment. Use purchase orders. Labor, as you know, is awfully expensive and you don't actually save money by not stocking; total cost can easily approach three times the base wage if you send a technician to purchase supplies. Their visits cost you money and decreases profit for the business.

A contractor wanted to save money by not buying anything until it was needed. He carried no inventory in his truck or in his shop. That's no inventory and no supplies for any job.

His technician would go to a job, make a list of what he needed for the job and then leave the job to go to a discount supplier. He would charge the supplies or equipment to a company account (in fact, the company had over 30 in-house accounts at various suppliers in the market). The technician would then drive back to the job, hoping he had all the parts he needed for the job.

Imagine repeating this process four to six times per day. I had to remind the contractor of the cost of labor to go get the parts, the cost of labor to return to the job and the price he was paying for parts.

Negotiate with your suppliers for lower costs and use just one or two suppliers to get the best pricing. The more suppliers you have the less leverage you have on pricing.

Another company I visited shopped pricing for all service parts. Once a technician knew what they needed, they called the "shoppers" in the company.

The shoppers then called three to five suppliers to locate the best price and relayed the information back to the technician. The technician then left the job, drove to the supply house, picked up the "cheapest" part and return to the job—again hoping he had everything he needed.

There were over 50 supply shops in town and the company shopped all of them. This was especially ironic because there was a supply house, with locations all over town, headquartered only 50 feet away from the company. I think they could have negotiated with this one major supplier and eliminated the time-consuming efforts of the shoppers.

Take advantage of discounts from suppliers. For example, if a supplier offers a 2% 10 / net 30 discount, that means that they'll give you a 2% discount if you pay within the first 10 days of invoice. They'll give you a 0% discount for the next 20 days. A company would lose 2% every 20 days, which equals 36% APR loss. Borrow the money for less than 36% APR and take the discounts.

Inventory Control

Inventory control is critical for success, but I've seen that many businesses don't bother to manage their inventory—they don't even put a value on their balance sheet. It's like they have no inventory.

To properly control inventory, you need to count inventory at the start of your fiscal year. The count must be based on one of these methods:

- FIFO (first in first out) cost
- LIFO (last in first out) cost
- Average cost

Once you choose the method for costing your inventory, you can't change. Most small businesses choose average inventory cost.

Let's say that on January 1, you count the inventory and find that you have a value of $10,000.

During January you purchase inventory for $20,000. Your total value of inventory is now $30,000.

Also in January, you sell $12,000 worth of inventory (value from costs of sales in materials and equipment). So on January 31, the inventory number on your balance sheet should read $30,000 - $12,000 = $18,000.

If you don't sell anything else on January 31, the inventory value on February 1 would be $18,000. January 31 rolls to February 1.

The same type of transactions would continue each month until you reach the end of your fiscal year.

Let's say that on December 31 your inventory is $22,000. On January 1 of the following year, you count and find you only have $17,000 worth of inventory. You're $5,000 short.

Why are you short? Maybe you miscounted. Maybe there was theft. Maybe someone didn't properly write down the inventory used. Regardless of the reason, you lost $5,000 of inventory.

This loss or adjustment to inventory would be placed on the profit & loss statement under variable overhead, unapplied materials.

Some clients tell me that it costs too much to control inventory. I am telling you that you *must* control inventory. It's up to the owner to set specific rules on how to check in and check out inventory because inventory costs more than most business owners think.

Consider the example we looked at above. A loss of $5,000 may not seem like much, but you're looking at the problem from a different point of view. The correct view is to divide your lost inventory by your net profit %. If this business lost $5,000 in inventory and made a 5% net profit, they would have to generate $100,000 more in sales to make up for the loss. It's easier to control inventory than it is to generate $100,000 more in sales.

If you're a service business, create an inventory list that will be carried on all your vehicles. Ask your distributor to provide the list for you. To get started, park all your service and installation vehicles on a Friday and inventory each one over the weekend. Take everything out of the vehicle that isn't attached to it. Put back in only those items on your inventory list. Require all employees to write down the parts they use each day and turn that list in to the office. At the end of each week, restock the trucks. Allow limited access to inventory and be sure to use the old items first. Don't let your employees stock their own vehicles. Even installation vehicles should be cleaned and restocked by warehouse personnel, not installers.

I remember helping one of my clients clean and inventory his service vehicles. He had all the service personnel come into the shop for a company meeting on a Friday afternoon. After a short meeting, he asked all the technicians to pass their truck keys up to the front of the room. There was a lot of dissent, but the owner said to not worry—he had organized office personnel and a rideshare app to take them home. If they had personal items in the truck, they were escorted to the truck to retrieve those items.

The technicians were instructed to return on Monday at 8:00 a.m. to retrieve their vehicles. Over the weekend, the 12 vehicles were going to get a thorough cleaning—inside and out—and we were going to perform an inventory check. After all personnel left the building, our team of eight—

me, the owner, his 10-year-old daughter and five of her friends—kicked off the process.

Our plan of attack was to take every single thing out of every single truck and place it on the warehouse floor, putting things that looked similar together. We left no stone unturned. Consoles, glove compartments, anything attached to the shades or laying on the dash—everything was fair game. I now know why service vehicles always seem to have front end alignment problems—because of all the weight on the dash!

We worked Friday afternoon, took the girls for pizza and then returned on Saturday morning to continue our work through the weekend. It was an interesting experience, to say the least.

Among other things, we found old invoices that had never been turned in and a lot of excess inventory. One truck had seven motors when it was only supposed to carry two. Another truck had six bottles of refrigerant when it only needed one. Overall, we found about $26,000 in excess inventory on the trucks.

Saving the best for last, one truck had invoices from a competitor under the front seat. Apparently the technician was using his truck to run service calls at night for the competitor. He was de-hired on Monday.

We reloaded the consoles and glove compartments with the proper paperwork, put Material Safety Data Sheets (MSDS) books behind the front seat of each vehicle and properly stocked them with the right inventory. The vehicles were thoroughly cleaned, serviced and ready to roll on Monday morning with the correct amount of stock.

From that moment forward, the technicians were required to write down all the inventory they used on jobs. Those items were restocked every Friday by office personnel. The client was able to substantially reduce his inventory by not letting his technicians stock their own trucks or go to supply houses. All inventory is now purchased through a purchase order system and inventory is measured weekly.

Labor

In addition to inventory, labor is probably the most expensive cost you have. You have labor costs in direct costs, variable overhead and fixed overhead.

You also have two types of workers, exempt and non-exempt, and you pay them differently. How you pay them can make all the difference to your bottom line, so let's explore how to structure labor payroll to give you extra dollars.

Direct Labor Costs

No other expense will be harder to control than direct labor. Throw out your Owner badge and put on your Manager of Labor badge and you'll save big time.

Remember, direct labor is the time spent on billable jobs. If the time can be linked to a customer, then the cost of labor goes in this category. If the cost is related to unbillable time, like training, then the cost goes in indirect variable overhead as unapplied (shop) time.

Direct labor is typically the people you have in the field doing the physical work. Direct labor personnel are hourly workers who are non-exempt employees. They must be paid overtime if they work over 8 hours per day or over 40 hours per week, depending on the state in which you reside. Timecards must be filled out completely, including breaks and lunch periods, and signed by the employee to be valid.

Overtime for direct labor, and perhaps for office personnel as well, is defined as 1.5 times the *average* hourly wage per pay period, not the *normal* hourly pay. The calculation that you need to use is:

total compensation for the period / total hours worked for the period

This is particularly important so let's look at some very specific examples.

Employee A works 40 hours per period and earns $800.

$800 / 40 hours = $20 per hour so overtime hours would be worth 1.5 times $20 or $30 / overtime hour. No overtime was worked, so total compensation would be $800.

Employee B works 50 hours per period and earns $20 per hour.

$1,000 / 50 hours = $20 per hour so overtime hours would be worth 1.5 times $20 or $30 / overtime hour. Since you've already paid the employee regular time ($20 per overtime hour), you need to give the employee an additional 10 hours overtime x ½ ($20) for a total of $100.

Forty hours were worked for $20 per hour and 10 hours were worked for $30 per hour. Total compensation would be $1,100.

Employee C works 50 hours per period and earns $20 per hour plus a bonus of $200.

Total compensation is $1,000 + $200 / 50 hours = $24 per hour so overtime is 1.5 times $24 or $36 per hour. Since you've already paid the employee regular time ($24 per overtime hour), you need to give the employee an additional 10 hours overtime x ½ ($24) or $120. Total compensation would be $1,320 which includes regular wages plus the bonus plus overtime.

Many large employers miss this critical function and I'm guessing that more than 80% of small businesses miss it. Just remember:

- Typically you must pay overtime for over 40 hours.
- You must adjust the overtime hourly rate based on the average rate (not the normal rate).
- Timecards must be completely filled out and signed.

QuickBooks and other payroll packages don't do this for you so you must manipulate the calculation correctly yourself.

It makes no difference whether you pay every week or every two weeks. Overtime is defined as working over 40 hours in a one week period. If you pay every two weeks and an employee works 50 hours one week and 30 hours the next week, for a total of 80 hours, you must pay them 10 hours overtime for the 50-hour week. In some states, overtime is even defined as over eight hours per day.

For more information about this critical calculation, visit the Department of Labor website at dol.gov/agencies/whd/overtime/fww.

Non-Exempt

Non-exempt employees are not exempt from overtime pay. You must pay them overtime as described above. Technicians, installers, field assistants and even most office workers (unless they manage someone) are usually non-exempt workers.

If you have any field labor, as in direct costs, their wages are directly billable to a customer. You may pay them $20 per hour but bill the customer $100 per hour. As we learned in the previous section, since these employees are hourly workers (meaning they are non-exempt from overtime) you must pay them for each normal hour worked and 1.5 times their average wage for overtime hours. The profit center (see Chapter 13 for a thorough explanation of profit centers) for labor will let you pay hourly workers in different ways, but you must equate their pay to an hourly wage.

You could pay field personnel two different hourly wages, say $20 for each billable hour and $15 for each unbillable hour, or you could pay field personnel a commission, but it must be divided by their hours worked to get an average hourly wage.

Timecards must be dated for the work period and must be signed to be valid. They should include fields for:

- Time in and out for each job
- Invoice or job number
- Total time worked
- Billable time
- Unapplied labor time

Exempt

Exempt employees don't receive overtime pay because they typically have an exemption. For example, sales personnel have a professional exemption, office managers have administrative exemptions and owners and managers have executive exemptions. All would be considered exempt employees.

When it comes to sales personnel, you could pay them a salary, salary plus commission or commission only. I recommend paying salary plus commission. Have them earn about 25–30% of their pay through salary, then the remainder on commission based on gross margin. The commission could be 10–15% of gross margin for the job.

Wage Matrix

Many employers use a salary or hourly matrix system for all employees. Create a spreadsheet like the one below for each profit center in your company.

Service Department

		1	2	3	4	5	6	7
E	Controls Tech	$20.00	$20.50	$21.00	$21.50	$22.00	$22.50	$23.00
D	Commercial Tech	$17.00	$17.50	$18.00	$18.50	$19.00	$19.50	$20.00
C	Residential Tech	$14.00	$14.50	$15.00	$15.50	$16.00	$16.50	$17.00
B	PTU Specialist	$11.00	$11.50	$12.00	$12.50	$13.00	$13.50	$14.00
A	Apprentice	$8.00	$8.50	$9.00	$9.50	$10.00	$10.50	$11.00

If you go to my website, collier-consulting.com, you can download a template for salesperson sales based on salary, monthly bonuses, quarterly bonuses and yearly bonuses.

Each profit center should have a matrix that goes with the job description (see Chapter 14). Most of my clients have about 10 of each. They hire non-exempt employees based on the job description and place them on the matrix.

Using the matrix above as an example, I could hire a residential technician and place them on C3 at $15 per hour.

Evaluate your employees every 90 days. Waiting for an employee to be in their position one year before they get a review is too long. At the end of the 90-day period, the employee gets a raise, a bonus or nothing. Most employers should follow the 80/20 rule where 80% of the workers get a bonus and 20% get a raise. If they have improved in their position, give them a raise. If they haven't improved or gotten better, give them a one-time bonus. If they aren't doing well, give them nothing and set standards for the next 90 days.

If the residential technician in the example above got a raise, I'd move their wage to C4, or $15.50 per hour. If they got a bonus, I'd give them 10 times their hourly wage. If they got nothing, they'd get $0 and the reasoning behind it.

Subcontractors

Direct subcontractors, also known as independent contractors, include companies owned by individuals that are independent of your company. As we learned earlier, subcontractors are the companies that you hire to do work for you. These are the factors to consider when working with subcontractors from the irs.gov website:

Facts that provide evidence of the degree of control and independence fall into three categories:

1. **Behavioral:** Does the company control or have the right to control what the worker does and how the worker does his or her job?

2. **Financial:** Are the business aspects of the worker's job controlled by the payer (these include things like how worker is paid, whether expenses are reimbursed, who provides tools/supplies, etc.)?

3. **Type of Relationship:** Are there written contracts or employee type benefits (i.e. pension plan, insurance, vacation pay, etc.)? Will the relationship continue and is the work performed a key aspect of the business?

If any of the above are true, your workers are more like employees than subcontractors.

Most of the time you can't provide things like training, tools, supplies, uniforms and hourly wages to subcontractors. They should look totally different than your employees. Have each subcontractor that you hire complete a subcontractor agreement each year, bill you for the job performed, and then you pay them with a check. Also create a file for each one with the agreement, copy of business cards, advertising and all invoices issued.

You as an employer are responsible for proving that a subcontractor isn't an employee. An independent contractor may not pay their income taxes and tell the IRS that you took the taxes out of their paycheck and you didn't send their tax money to the IRS. Just be careful hiring independent contractors who represent your company. How does your insurance treat them? What responsibility do you have to your customers if something bad happens?

Other Direct Costs

Other direct costs include miscellaneous fees on jobs and warranty work done under warranty. Do you get reimbursed under warranty? How long does it take your company to submit a warranty claim and how often do you receive reimbursement? Also, be sure to make all invoices numeric then deduct the warranty credit to show the customer how much it would have cost them on all invoices you issue. Other direct costs must be billable to a specific job.

Controlling Indirect Variable Overhead

Indirect variable overhead includes those costs that tend to vary with sales. If sales go up, they go up, if sales go down, they go down. Look carefully at each cost and see if you can trim them.

Advertising

Be sure you're measuring your advertising cost and the return on investment (cost of advertising / profit generated). A great example of variable advertising is Facebook—you can adjust your spend or turn it off completely on a regular basis. I call this category turn-on/turn-off advertising because the costs are typically short-term.

Auto and Truck Maintenance

Do you have good tires and maximize fuel performance? Do you have a regular maintenance schedule?

Auto and Truck Gas and Oil

Do you have a corporate fuel credit card? Do employees have to enter mileage to get gas? Who pays for car washes? Who pays for oil? Do you charge for use of your truck for personal use? Are vehicles really used 100% of the time for business? Do you deduct 100% vehicle use on your tax return?

Bad Debts

Do you have a written collection policy? Do you charge interest on accounts or do you have a billing charge? Do you send past due invoices?

Equipment Expense

Do you lease equipment or is it purchased? Renegotiate maintenance agreements on equipment.

Freight

How are items shipped to your business? Check to see if you can lower shipping charges by buying larger quantities or changing providers.

Interest and Bank Charges

Renegotiate loans and manage bank charges. Banks should not be charging you a service fee. Think about how much they make off of your deposits.

Miscellaneous

This category should be less than 1% of sales. It should only be used for abnormal spending.

Office Expenses

Check your office supplies like paper and toner. Be aware: there are many phone and internet scams that will try to take advantage of your office personnel.

Payroll Taxes

These are related to payroll expenses, so be sure to check all time-cards and reduce overtime as much as possible. Remember that you, the business owner, control overtime. Employees should not work overtime without your permission or their manager's permission.

Sales Commissions

Save on sales commissions by giving salespeople a flat rate instead of a percent of sales. A salesperson might sell something at a loss, but you still have to pay them. Base commissions on gross margins, not on sales.

Shop Supplies and Tools

Don't allow technicians to purchase tools, but do allow them to earn credit for tools at your local supplier. Issue purchase orders for all tools—and only purchase tools that are actually needed.

Travel and Entertainment

All travel for business-related activities (air travel to attend training, vehicle mileage to call on customers, etc.) is 100% deductible. Business-related meals and entertainment for employees and for customers and potential customers is also deductible. Some businesses use separate credit cards for travel and entertainment.

Unapplied Labor

These are the wages paid for unbillable time (billable wages are in direct labor). You want this value to be as close to zero as possible. For example, if a service technician works 40 hours per week, you want most of the labor wage billed to a customer. If you can't bill the customer for the time, the time goes here. Most companies don't split labor as they should—it's not uncommon for this value to be 20% or more for service companies.

Unapplied Materials

I call this *costs of goods gone*. These are the materials, supplies and equipment that you've bought that are now missing. You have no idea where they are. This is sometimes the value of what you thought you had versus what you actually had. If you thought your inventory was worth $300 and you only counted $200, then the missing inventory goes here at a value of $100.

Vacation, Holiday and Bonus Pay

This is what you pay for vacation days, holidays or job performance. If you give your employees an end-of-year bonus, separate from normal payroll, it would go here.

Controlling Indirect Fixed Overhead

Fixed overhead expenses are those that typically don't change much as sales change. Rent doesn't change as sales go up or down. Utilities don't change much as well. We budget these expenses in dollars and not percentage of sales. Let's review a few of the more important categories.

Advertising

Fixed advertising costs don't change often. Think about your website or your subscription to the Yellow Pages, trade magazines or community newspapers. Evaluate your advertising with metrics and measure every sale. Where did the sale come from? If you divide the net profit from those sales by the costs of advertising for those sales, you get return on investment. If my website costs me $1,000 per month and I want a 20% return on investment, I need to generate a profit of $200. If my profit percent from sales is 10%, then I need to generate $2,000 in sales from the advertising. Beware of persons who use sales in the equation. One might say if you spend $1,000 and get $2,000 in sales, that is a 200% return on investment. Totally incorrect, so be careful.

Employee Benefits

Employee benefits is usually a large number in the fixed overhead category. This might include insurance and 401k contributions.

I want to address insurance. Insurance, such as health and life insurance, should be a shared expense. If you, as an employer, pay 100% of the premium, the employee doesn't know the actual cost—the value that you provide for them. When you split the premium with the employee in some fashion, they pay more and know the true costs of insurance if the rates go up. And if the rates do go up, which they almost certainly will, you're not paying all of the increase.

In my work with one company, I discovered that a group of employees thought medical insurance cost the company about $50 per month per employee—but in reality it was more than $200 per employee.

Be transparent with insurance cost information so that employees recognize the value of the benefit.

Owner's Salary

This is always found in fixed overhead—and it should be substantial. Always pay yourself a paycheck every single week that you work. Don't just take draws when you need them. The business needs to know that this expense is going to be consistent and constant. If you can't pay yourself, why pay employees? If the business can't pay you a salary, is the business a hobby? Does your significant other work for free? Most service company owners pay themselves at least 8% of sales plus benefits, and if the business improves they take quarterly bonuses or distributions from their corporation.

Summary

Controlling costs in a company requires diligence from the owner and managers.

Examine the expenses each month and be sure that they're in line with the norm. Look at percentage of sales for direct costs and indirect variable overhead to see if you notice any major shifts. Review how much you're spending for fixed overhead.

Remember, your greatest cost is labor. Watch the hours on all time-cards and pre-approve overtime hours. Most field service businesses that I encounter have about 20% more field workers than they need. If you have 20 field workers and they're only billing 60% of their time, it's like having 12 field workers billing 100% of their time. If you become the Manager of Labor in your company, your costs will dramatically decrease and your profits will soar.

CHAPTER 12

CREATING CUSTOMERS FOR LIFE

"Instead of focusing on the competition, focus on the customer."

—Scott Cook

n the last chapter we talked about controlling the costs associated with a business and how the major cost in any organization is labor. When you add up all the truck expenses, payroll, benefits, insurance and so much more, you can easily see why labor consumes most of the expenses. It isn't that you don't need labor, it's just that you just don't need too much labor to take care of you most valuable asset—your customer.

Think about the value of a company. I value companies all the time and, while they all have assets that can be sold, most buyers can purchase those assets elsewhere. The only real assets in a business are customers and goodwill. It's hard to buy customers and it's difficult to measure goodwill.

About 20 years ago, a heating, ventilation and air conditioning client of mine wanted to expand. I told him to start by looking for a business to buy. It takes a lot of money to start, or even expand, a business, but an existing business already has assets, organization, a company name and customers. Why not buy a proven business where most of the work has already been done?

I suggested that he call every heating, ventilation and air conditioning company in the phone book and make note of those that were out of business. He followed my instructions and found seven that were defunct.

Next I told him to go to the county records and find the owners of those businesses, contact them ask them if they had sold their assets and if he could schedule a private meeting with them.

Upon completing this task, he called me back and said he had found one that had sold about $300,000 worth of installations and service. The owner had just grown older and closed his business. I told him to schedule an appointment and I would attend the meeting with him.

On the day of the meeting, I asked my client to stop by the bank on his way and withdraw $10,000 cash.

The owner was great, and we enjoyed hearing about how he had started the business with his son. In the end, however, he couldn't do enough work to sustain both of them. The son wasn't necessarily pulling his weight in accordance with the pay he was given. The owner had finally shut the doors because he couldn't do all the work and he was too tired to continue.

The only assets we wanted were the owner's company name, phone number and customer files (in this case, three filing cabinets out in his garage). My client started counting out cash until they reached an agreement. We walked away that night with the assets we wanted and everyone was happy. Customers are key. As I have said in my workshops, "Businesses go out of business every day, but service stickers, business cards, decals and phone numbers just keep on going."

My client forwarded the phone number to his office, sent letters to the customers that had been with the other company for over 20 years and, because of the purchase, increased his overall business about $200,000 the first year.

Great companies don't want customers to buy just one item, they want customers to buy multiple items multiple times. Think about Amazon and you'll understand how this should work in your business.

Understand Marketing Verses Advertising

Before we launch into the creating Customers for Life program for your company, let's differentiate between marketing and advertising.

Marketing is everything you say and do that effects a customer's desire to purchase from you. Lettered service trucks, signs, brochures, ads, uniforms on field personnel, letterhead, answering the phones and quality of personnel are many of the things in your business that influence how customers make the decision to buy (or not buy, as the case may be). You want to constantly market to customers because you're building your image and the value that image conveys.

Advertising is just promoting your product. For example, placing an ad for a service in a newspaper or on a website is advertising, not promotion, of your image.

You may have heard that marketing follows these three rules:

- Expectation
- Experience
- Evaluation

You want to measure all three to see how well you did and measure the potential for future sales. Imagine, for a moment, that you are a restaurant owner...

What does a customer **expect** from your restaurant? Do they expect a nice location, easy parking, friendly greeters, nice atmosphere, quality service, good food, acceptable prices, clean space, well mixed drinks and lots of choices? Yes to all of these. As a restaurant owner, do you provide all of these and meet the customer's expectations?

Next, look at the customer's **experience** at your restaurant. Did your restaurant provide great food, incredible service, beautifully laid tables, professional servers and valet parking?

To get the evaluation for your restaurant, you'd use this formula:

Expectation x Experience = Evaluation

Let's say I expected seven things from your restaurant, one of which was convenient parking. When I arrived, you actually provided me with free valet parking—a step above convenient parking. If I expected a seven and you gave me an eight, my evaluation would be 56. You would have exceeded my expectations.

As I was preparing to return home from a business trip, I got a phone call from my wife. She confirmed that she'd pick me up from the Dallas airport as planned, but that we'd stop for dinner with our friends JR and Jean on the way home. I made a reservation at a new restaurant near the airport; we'd heard that they served great food.

When we arrived at the restaurant, we were immediately greeted by the hostess. She told us our table would be ready in just a few minutes and she took our drink orders while we waited. She served us those drinks before we were seated—an experience that made us feel like celebrities, and it was a great way for the restaurant to make more money.

When we arrived at our beautifully laid table, the attendant seated us at the appropriate place—at each of our place settings there was a small place card printed with our name. JR definitely thought I was buddies with the owner because he gave me both the thumbs up and the OK sign. It was an incredibly nice touch from the restaurant, but I had arranged nothing.

Then I remembered that when I had called to make the reservation, I was asked who would be joining my wife and I for dinner. I gave them the names of our guests and thought nothing more about it. But wow, what a special, personal touch!

That night was full of fabulous food, superior service and wonderful drinks, but when JR brought up that night out on the town over the years, he always mentioned that small piece of cardboard, a simple place card.

Think about my entire restaurant experience. Your company should:

- List the customer's expectations

- Review those expectations with the team

- Determine how you're going to exceed those expectations and provide the customers with the experience they're looking for

Consider assembling a customer focus group to bring customers in to discuss their expectations and what you as a company did and didn't deliver. Follow-up with a customer after a sale. Look at your online reviews. Do you like what you see?

Many years ago, a pizza chain sent my family a letter inviting us to be "mystery shoppers." We were to go to one of their locations and order an appetizer, drinks, entrees and even dessert. They would reimburse us for the entire meal if we submitted our receipt and a completed questionnaire. The questionnaire was extensive—we were really surprised. They asked about restaurant and food temperature, cars in the parking lot, greeters, time to take the order, time to get the order, cleanliness, attitude and probably 50 more things. The questions were well thought out because they reflected the customer's experience.

My children loved the entire process. My daughter took notes on the questionnaire while my son gave her all the facts. They were serious. The company even praised us for our great responses.

One night as we were sitting in another restaurant, my son took out a stopwatch that he had purchased with his own money. He felt they needed to time procedures more accurately, to the "hundredth" of a second. Both my kids loved that a company would allow us to evaluate their restaurants—and of course we all loved the free food.

I suggest that all companies have a "mystery shopper" or a panel of shoppers. Emails and online reviews typically don't get to the real heart of the like or dislike for a company. Ask customers specifically if you met or exceeded their expectations and why. Get feedback at least once per quarter on how your company is doing overall.

As a company, you need to think about treating your customers well by creating an awesome expectation, delivering an exceptional experience and scoring a super evaluation. This will generate more referrals and more business.

Exercise

What do you think customers expect from your business?

What do you think your customers actually experience?

What do you do after the evaluation to gain more of their business and referrals?

Use the Customers for Life Model (CFL)

Ron Smith, the author of *HVAC Spells Wealth*, ran a phenomenally successful air conditioning company for many years. His model talks about follow-up and the importance of keeping in contact with the customer. The more contacts, the more touches, the greater the chance for more sales.

The Customers for Life model starts with someone buying a product or service from you. You created a great website, a great expectation, and the customer answers with a sale. Now what?

If you order from Amazon, you immediately receive a receipt for the product. Soon you receive a notice that they're preparing the item for shipping, which is followed by a notice that the product has shipped. After the product arrives you get another notice about the actual delivery.

See how many times they "touched" you? There is no way you could have forgotten about Amazon and the product they sold you.

The Customers for Life model must include immediate follow-up and continued interaction with the customer. Let's look at how the model would work in real life. Imagine for a moment that you're the customer…

1.   You call a company for service and make an appointment.

2.   The company calls back to confirm the appointment.

3.   They send a service technician to your home.

4.   After the repair, the technician offers you a service agreement to

maintain your equipment with discounts on future repairs.

5. You receive a call/email from the company asking how the initial contact was, how the service call went and your satisfaction with the technician. I call this a "happy call."

6. A few months later you receive a call/email to schedule a maintenance call. You call the company back and schedule the appointment.

7. The company calls the day after the appointment with another "happy call."

All this repeats itself over and over and over.

Sell a product. Track the product. Deliver the product. Make a happy call. Call or email again. Sell a product. Track the product. Deliver the product. Make a happy call. You do this over and over again to keep the customers close to you.

The problem with most small businesses is that they don't follow-up and don't have a plan for Customers for Life. You get one sale and that's it. No happy calls, no follow-up, no opportunities. If you remember the customer, they will remember you.

One of my clients has a heating, ventilation and air conditioning company that sells and installs heating and air conditioning equipment. After they replace a furnace or air conditioner, they contact Cookie Advantage who sends a custom tin of chocolate chip cookies to the customer with a thank you card from the owner and a survey card to see how well they performed. The customers get cookies and the company gets immediate, personal feedback.

Develop Your Plan

Just like with other procedures in your business, which we'll discuss in detail in Chapter 15, have a written plan for what to do to get the sale, monitor the sale, follow-up on the sale and generate new sales. You don't just want sales from your customers—you want sales from their family, friends and neighbors as well. If you can get referrals and repeat business, the sales generated are typically at higher margins.

Get Out

You also need to get out of your office. Not a lot of business is generated in a small business from your office. You might be a member of the Chamber of Commerce but don't go to meetings. Maybe you're in Rotary but never attend. Part of Customers for Life is being out in the community that you need to support you.

Customers are a lot like people. First they have to know who you are. Then they must respect and admire you, believing that you're a good person who runs an honest business. If these things are true to a customer, they will buy from you once—and the service or product you provide during that first sale will determine whether they buy from you again. How many times do we go back to a bad restaurant? Zero. The same is true for a business.

Have a definitive plan and stick to it. Measure your leads to see which are the most effective and invest more in those with the greatest return.

Generate Leads

Put someone in charge of marketing in your company. Most small business owners are too busy to market effectively, and most owners don't know how to properly market in the first place. Set aside at least 3% of sales for marketing, maybe even 5% if you're just starting out. Many customers don't know you exist, so explore the many options you have available to tell your story.

If you send out a marketing piece, let's say direct mail, you'll reach three kinds of people:

- Active customers (bought from you in the last 12 months)
- Inactive customer (bought from you, but longer than 12 months ago)
- Non-customers (have never bought from you)

You'll get leads from all of them, but your active customers are five to seven times more likely to buy from you than a non-customer. Inactive customers are three times more likely to buy than a non-customer. It costs you about $220–$403 to convert a non-customer to an active one.

Most small businesses tend to focus on the non-customer instead of the active and inactive customers, but that's not the best approach. If you have $1,000 to spend, put $500 toward active customers, $300 toward inactive customers and $200 toward non-customers. The same is true for emailing customers and Facebook marketing.

Manage Customer Files

Too many businesses have paper files for their customers. These aren't easily sorted to send emails, letters or text messages as part of a Customers for Life plan. I've seen businesses with 10–20 file cabinets stuffed with paper. One company I worked with had a computer folder with scanned documents for each customer. They had over 6,000 folders and each folder had 10–60 scanned documents. What are you going to do with that?!?

Turn your customer information into useable files and develop a specific plan to follow-up a sale, a solicitation for a sale or a reminder for service or specials. Target your active customer base and have them grow your business. Using customer management software, as we discussed in Chapter 3, will be a key part of these processes.

Summary

This was not a marketing chapter from a marketing book. There are many great books on marketing (some of my favorites are from Jay Conrad Levinson). This was a chapter to emphasize the importance of customers and their relationship with you. Marketing books will tell you how to get leads and maybe turn them into customers, but Customers For Life shows you what to do with them after they become customers.

CHAPTER 13

ORGANIZING FOR SUCCESS

"Organization isn't about perfection. It's about efficiency, reducing stress and clutter, saving time and money, and improving your overall quality of life."

—*Christina Scalise*

In the previous chapter we talked about how to take care of customers before, during and after a sale. Great companies focus on the customer and their needs and provide the products and services that satisfy those needs. If you have the products and services to meet those needs, but the customer doesn't know it, they won't buy. It's up to you to make sure that the customer is informed.

In this chapter, we're going to focus on how to organize your company for success. We'll discuss your organizational chart and profit centers.

Add Names to Your Organizational Chart

An organizational chart with just one name—your name—means your business is a one-man shop. At this stage in business you're called an owner because you have no employees to manage. Once you hire an employee (or employees) and you add names to the organizational chart, you become a business. You're then called an owner/manager. A business will become an organization once a manager is hired.

If you're a one-man shop, you're wearing the technician hat. If you're a business, you're wearing the manager hat. If you're an organization, you're wearing the entrepreneur hat.

From day one, you should produce—and maintain—an organizational chart. This chart should be distributed to everyone employed by the company to show the hierarchy of roles, and specifically who is in charge of each profit center and its employees. This chart should become part of your employee manual and distributed yearly to all employees.

Without an organizational chart, there is no definitive supervisor or boss. Employee feedback tells us that this causes a lot of problems from the start. All employees must know who they report to and who can hire and de-hire them. If my manager can't de-hire me, why do I have to do what they say?

Most successful businesses that I work with have about five people reporting to one person, which is usually the right amount for an individual to manage.

Create Profit Centers

How can you measure the effectiveness and efficiency of your managers? The best way is to set up profit centers for your companies. I want to emphasize the importance of "profit" in any business. I'm going to judge my managers based on the profit they generate. If they make money, you should reward them. If they lose money, then why do you employ them? You could do that yourself.

Most companies have trouble setting up and evaluating their profit centers, so we're going to go through an example on how it's done.

Company		Installation	Service
Sales	$500,000	300,000	200,000
MESO	$200,000	150,000	50,000
Labor	$100,000	75,000	25,000
Gross Margin	$200,000	75,000	125,000
Overhead	$164,000	???	???
Profit	$36,000	???	???

If I had two managers working for me and I was going to evaluate them on their respective profit centers, installation and service, how would I measure their success? To me, success is defined by profitability, but what is the profitability of their profit centers?

Most companies don't have a standard way to allocate or distribute overhead to the profit centers to get a true profit picture.

Some companies allocate overhead as a percentage of sales, but that isn't correct. In this example, since installation is 60% of sales,

I would allocate 60% of the overhead to the install profit center. It doesn't work.

Other companies allocate overhead as a percentage of MESO or labor, but that isn't a good way to allocate it either. There's no direct link between MESO or labor and sales. Just because MESO goes up, it doesn't mean overhead goes up.

If you use sales, MESO or labor to distribute overhead, you'll either under allocate or over allocate overhead and not get a true value. Labor comes close and that's what many accountants use, but it's still not the best.

So what is the best method to allocate overhead? It's called dual overhead allocation. In Chapter 9 we used dual overhead allocation to calculate the direct breakeven on jobs and then we added profit. That gave us the best method to determine the correct price, and it also gives us the best method to allocate overhead to profit centers.

In the example company above, the dual overhead calculations revealed 1.20 for labor and 0.22 for MESO. We'll use these calculations for our profit centers.

If we multiply 1.20 times the labor for installation, we get $90,000 for labor overhead for this profit center. If we multiply 0.22 times MESO of $150,000, we get $33,000 for MESO overhead for this profit center. If we add these together, we get $123,000 total overhead for installation. Total overhead for installation is $123,000 and total overhead for service is $41,000.

Now look at our profit centers when overhead is properly applied:

Company		Installation	Service
Sales	$500,000	300,000	200,000
MESO	$200,000	150,000	50,000
Labor	$100,000	75,000	25,000
Gross Margin	$200,000	75,000	125,000
Overhead	$164,000	123,000	41,000
Profit	$36,000	(48,000)	84,000

Check out what happened when we properly allocated overhead. Installation lost money and service made money. Even though installation had the most sales, it lost the most money. Now we can easily evaluate and measure the profit center and its manager.

Summary

In this chapter we discussed how profit centers can help you, as an owner, control the different facets of your business. You need to learn how to properly break your company into manageable bits. Assign a budget and run profit & loss statements with overhead distribution each month. Measure your managers on gross margin or profit, not sales, unless you set the specific sale point.

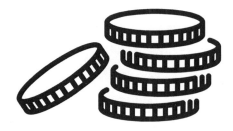

CHAPTER 14

HIRING RIGHT THE FIRST TIME

*"We focus on two things when hiring. First, find the best
people you can in the world, and second, let them do
their work. Just get out of their way."*

—*Matt Mullenweg*

I n the last chapter we discussed the importance of hiring managers and giving them profit centers to manage. This is how you'll measure their effectiveness and efficiency. All managers and employees should be rewarded based on performance, not just time on the job.

Most businesses need to put a sign on their door that says, "Hiring qualified personnel." The reasons for this are twofold:

1. Your competitors will think you're growing and becoming more of player in the marketplace.

2. Your employees will see that you're always looking for better personnel.

One common problem in the hiring process is that business owners don't have a good grasp of the job they need to fill, much less the person they need to fill the job.

Your business can't grow without employees. If you don't grow, you'll continue to be stuck wearing the technician hat. You must hire, give part of your job to a new employee and let go of some responsibility. Hire people to do what you don't want to do or what you're not capable of doing, and be sure that you know what the person is going to do before starting the hiring process.

Write Job Descriptions

There should be a job description for each role in each of your profit centers (office, service, installation, maintenance, etc.). Don't hire anyone into a job without a thorough job description for the role they'll fill.

Carefully prepared job descriptions show the hiring manager and the applicant what the job is all about and they outline your expectations for the position.

The job description will cover skill level, but it's up to you to make sure that you hire a productive person who wants to do the work. You may find someone who can process accounts payables, but you need to feel confident that's what they'll do all day—not just an hour or two here and there when they're taking a break from playing solitaire online .

You can start to determine things like an individual's productivity level and attitude during the interview.

Interview Effectively

You'll can learn a lot about a potential hire during the interview process, including their attitudes towards work, teamwork, life and the way they present themselves to the world, among other things. You'll see things that are part of their nature, and things they've been coached on over the course of their life. These things will indicate how they're going to approach their job.

I remember visiting one of my clients and asking how many service technicians the company had. He said that he had five and three quarters. I asked about the three quarters guy, Frank.

My client said Frank was not a morning person. Frank had gotten into lots of situations with customers, so he just let him come in when he wanted and leave when he wanted.

Frank had told the owner that he was not a "morning person," and would only work part of the day.

Another one of my clients had a salesperson named Bill. Nice guy, the owner said, but his personal hygiene was lacking. There had been complaints from several of his customers. Bill was costing the company plenty of money and referrals.

One of my clients looks at the potential hire's vehicle before making a final offer. He believes that the company vehicle would be kept as clean as the potential hire's personal vehicle.

Be sure each applicant fills out a hard copy application on-site—even if the initial application is done online. Don't let an applicant take the application home to complete because someone else may fill it out for them.

If you aren't familiar with the legal guidelines that need to be followed during the interview process, do some research well before the interview. Always make sure you're in line with the law.

Pre-Hire

You could also consider running a personality or behavioral assessment like DiSC, MBTI or DrakeP3 before making an offer in order to see how your potential hire may fit within the existing team. This will give you a deeper understanding of the individual right off the bat. If you don't take this step pre-hire, you'll almost certainly want to take it post-hire. An awareness of behavior and communication preferences is golden.

It's important to hire right the first time, so you may want to seek outside help if this isn't one of your strengths. Paul Vishnesky runs *Hire Dimensions*, an organization that handles many aspects of hiring. They offer personality/behavior assessments and even a bootcamp.

Another part of the pre-hire process is getting your new hire to sign a non-disclosure, non-solicitation agreement. Note that this isn't a non-compete. It's an agreement that prevents an employee from disclosing confidential information about the business and prevents them from contacting your customers directly. You must remember that it only takes one flash drive or a few screen grabs for someone to get all your company information.

Develop a Procedure Manual

Once an employee is hired, they should be given a procedure manual for the specific job they've been hired to do. This manual spells out for the employee the exact processes and procedures that your company expects them to follow—which may be a far cry from the way they have done things in the past. The procedure manual should be the basis for your new hire training. We'll discuss how to create this manual in the next chapter.

Manage Goals

Once you've hired the person that fits the job description, you need to manage their performance. Set goals and track their progress. Employee goals should be SMART goals. SMART is an acronym for:

- Specific
- Measurable
- Agreeable
- Reachable
- Timely

We would typically set a goal that sounds like this: *I want to lose weight*. But that isn't a SMART goal. There's nothing specific to measure and there's no time attached. A SMART goal sounds like this: *I will lose 20 pounds in the next three months*.

- Specific: Lose 20 pounds
- Measurable: Weigh now, and then again in three months
- Agreeable: You have buy-in/commitment
- Reachable: It's not so difficult that it can't be obtained
- Timely: Three months

If we give employees incomplete goals or goals that can't be measured, there's no accountability. How will we determine whether or not they are effective?

Many business owners allow employees to set their own goals and manage their own performance. No wonder we have so much trouble with employees! This approach allows for bad behavior.

You want each employee's manager to meet with them once per quarter to discuss their performance and how they're progressing with their goals. Most companies have these discussions just once or twice per year (if that), and at that point, it's too late. Performance discussions should be a regular part of your business.

One of my clients said, "I can't find good people." Maybe he should have said "I can't find a good owner." Many business owners blame the employee for performance issues, never themselves for giving incomplete or non-measurable tasks.

Be sure that you use SMART goals for your own objectives too.

Manage Time

Time Coming & Going

You don't have to pay employees for their commuting expenses.

Whether you furnish them with a truck or not, you start to pay them after they reach the primary or secondary job location. A primary job location would be the office or their first service call or installation. A secondary job location would be a supplier or a distributor, if the technician absolutely has to stop there.

Time stops when you tell the employee to go home for the day.

Overtime will kill a business. You, as a business owner, control overtime. If a non-exempt (hourly) worker comes to work at 6:00 a.m. and makes coffee, cleans his truck and visits with his friends in another department before getting started, he must still be paid starting at 6:00 a.m.

Management Time

In the book *Managing Management Time* by William Oncken, Oncken stressed that we can control employees' time, but we first need to manage our own time.

He used the "monkey on your back" approach by saying that you can't take care of your monkeys and those of your employees as well. As a manager, you only have so much time in a day to do what you need to do, never mind handle the jobs and responsibilities of your employees.

Don't take on other peoples' monkeys. You're a leader, not a carrier of monkeys. Do your job and expect others to do theirs. If you keep doing the work of other people, you won't have time to do yours. Give your team direction and back off.

Follow the Rules When De-Hiring

There are rules and regulations when it comes to releasing individuals from your employ. Among other things, this can include verbal warnings and clear guidelines in your employee manual. Make sure you're well versed on the laws in your state and comply accordingly. Always make sure you're in line with the law.

Summary

Ask yourself why you have employees and determine exactly how many you need. Most companies I have worked with have too few employees in the office and too many employees in the field. Look at how efficient your employees are, not how many hours they work.

Employees are hired to do what you don't want to do or what you aren't capable of doing.

Hire employees that share your vision and someone who wants a career, not a job. Take plenty of time to hire, and not long to de-hire.

Measure the impact your employees have on your company every

90 days. Give more bonuses than raises.

Employees are very expensive, but they are necessary for growth. Just be smart in hiring.

CHAPTER 15

FRANCHISING YOUR BUSINESS

"Consistent action creates consistent results."

—*Christine Kane*

I n the last chapter we discussed the hiring and maintenance of personnel. As business owners, we're always on the lookout for good people. We can usually find a place for the right person. If we hire correctly, our hope is that the employee will stay with us for many years, helping us succeed in our quest for profitability.

But hiring is only part of the challenge. We then need to guide employees to honor the business's way of doing business. We must teach them how to consistently do what we expect them to do. I use the word consistent because that is exactly what national franchises do, and you should aim to do the same.

Sell Consistency

Ask any restaurant owner if consistency is important. Ask any landscape company if consistency is important. Ask any business if consistency is important and the answer will be yes. It's yes because customers can't stand inconsistency.

We purchase from companies that deliver a consistent product or service, and we're likely to refer those companies to friends or relatives. To be successful in business you need to be consistent in the way you do things.

The downfall of many companies is that they don't give clear direction to their employees. Many companies never train their employees on how to do things the company way. Everyone is doing what they think is best for them—which is not necessarily what is best for the company.

For the best, most consistent performance, ensure that all employees follow your company's procedure manuals religiously. If everyone follows a procedure manual, systems are controlling personnel. This is ideal because there's not enough time in the day for you to monitor the consistency of all your personnel.

A client told me a story about hiring a service technician. The technician had great work experience, so he was hired on the spot and was to report for work the next day. The service technician reported on time wearing a white t-shirt, denim shorts and sneakers. My client was furious and demanded to know what this service technician's problem was. The technician told him that's the way they dressed at his previous employer so he thought that this was the way he should dress for his new employer.

See, the problem wasn't with the technician. The problem was with my client. He didn't establish a clear, written dress code. We don't want our employees to make assumptions about what they should do or wear. We need to tell them exactly what to do or wear.

Create Systems Like a Franchise Does

Most of you reading this book aren't going to take your company and its product or service and sell it as a franchise. However, franchising your company to your employees makes sense if it gives them clear direction.

Most franchises are purchased because they have a proven track record of success, using the tools and procedures that have worked for years and years. Your business should be structured like a franchise, but only to your employees.

You want to establish definitive procedures and use tools as systems to measure employees. If you make things automatic in your company, then employees can't change them. They have a specific, defined way of doing things. Franchises don't let employees regulate the temperature or time on fryers. Franchises don't let employees fill cups manually. They create systems that take the guesswork out of those decisions so that consistency prevails.

Think of a refrigerator as a system. Some things, like the light, are automatically controlled. The light comes on when you open the door and it shuts off when you close the door. It's an automatic response.

Think of online shopping as a system. When you order a product online, you put in your credit card information. If you don't put in all the correct information, the system won't let you place your order. You can hit submit five million times and your order still won't be processed. The system is controlling the process. If you don't follow the process correctly, you won't be able to complete your order.

Sticky notes, for example, are not a system. Sticky notes are temporary reminders to do something. When I walk in to evaluate a company, I tear up their sticky notes. Obviously, nothing on a sticky note is so valuable that you would stick it to the computer screen of just one employee. Obviously something on a sticky note isn't important enough to put into a procedure manual. Procedures are written down and shared with all employees.

Create Procedures

Procedure documents, also called desktop procedures (DTPs) or work instruction guides (WIGs), spell out the specific actions that your company expects an employee to take. The procedure manual, which is made up of desktop procedures for each task performed, is how you will evaluate an employee to see if they're doing the job correctly.

You should have a specific desktop procedure for each and every task such as:
- How to process accounts payables
- How to process accounts receivables
- How to order parts

- How to dispatch a service call
- How to issue a credit
- How to open the store

In order to successfully train your employees, each task that you'll teach them to perform should have a desktop procedure to support it. They can refer back to this when they're on their own after training is complete.

Each desktop procedure shows exactly how the company wants things done. Most procedures should be written so that a 12-year-old could perform the task. Take a look at this example for printing barcodes from an inventory system:

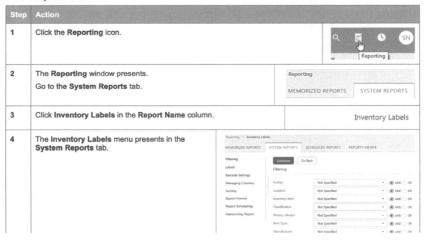

Generate, Print & Affix Barcodes: Part 2

Now that you have the list of items your site orders regularly, follow this process to generate the barcode labels that you will affix to your shelves.

Step	Action	
1	Click the **Reporting** icon.	
2	The **Reporting** window presents. Go to the **System Reports** tab.	
3	Click **Inventory Labels** in the **Report Name** column.	
4	The **Inventory Labels** menu presents in the **System Reports** tab.	

For a desktop procedure template that you can use in your business, visit the resources page at sarakeeney.com.

Exercise

Write a desktop procedure laying out how you would (1) go from wherever you are now to your kitchen and (2) make a cup of coffee or tea. Be detailed, specific, and make it clear enough for a 12-year-old. You can even draw images if you'd like.

Include desktop procedures for absolutely everything in your manual, even things that might seem to go without saying.

For example, if you're developing a procedure manual for the perfect service call, cover everything from the time the technician gets the call, to where they park, to how they approach the house, to how they greet the customer, to how they enter the house, to what they do during the call itself, to how they leave the call. If you want all old material removed from the jobsite and disposed of (not stuffed in the attic, which is what happened at my house) include that in your procedure. Direct the technician to train the customer on the use of their new product. Or if you have a YouTube video or other resource that shows the customer how to properly operate the new product, include instructions for sharing that with the customer in your procedure as well. Define dress codes.

Best practices must be specifically defined for each procedure. Employees should know exactly how to properly fulfill their role in the company and they should not deviate from the procedures that you provide. Show them how the company defines professionalism and give them a direct road to success.

When your procedure changes, be sure to update your documentation and share it with employees.

Track Employees

You should know where your employees are and what they're doing almost down to the minute. They're working for you, using your assets and providing service (or no service) to your customers. But how do you stay on top of where they at all times?

The customer relationship management programs covered in Chapter 3 can do this for salespeople. Dispatch software, combined with GPS on all company vehicles, can do this with field personnel.

Dispatch software will allow you to track all calls coming into the business so that you have a permanent record. You'll also know stop, start, departure and arrival times. Many companies also use this to provide payroll information. I recommend that all field personnel, including installers, technicians and sales personnel be dispatched and tracked. Dispatch only one call at a time (the primary problem with callbacks is too many calls at one time) and ensure that technicians track their times and close their tickets before they go to the next call.

And remember, put the GPS on the trucks, not on the phones. It's more important to locate a truck than it is to locate a phone. With a GPS on every truck and a program like @ROAD, you can track your trucks in real time online.

One of my clients saved over $1,400 a month on gas by just putting GPS on all his field trucks.

Another client put an empty box with wires coming out of it under the hood of each truck and saved over $300 per month on gas. The technicians assumed it was GPS!

In both cases, the technicians spent less time at lunch, were more efficient as they moved from service call to service call and quit taking the trucks out for personal use.

Summary

In this chapter I've addressed the importance of consistency in business. No matter what kind of business you are, consistency makes you a better company. Customers like good consistency—and they may tolerate bad consistency—but they can't stand inconsistency.

If you don't have a detailed procedure manual for each profit center in your business, then the employee is setting the standard, not the company. You'll find yourself with 50 employees doing things 50 different ways. If you haven't already started, get to work creating a procedure manual for each of your profit centers. Start by writing down the tasks that are needed in each profit center and you'll be on your way to consistency.

CHAPTER 16

PLANNING YOUR FUTURE

"Planning is bringing the future into the present so that you can do something about it now."

—Alan Lakein

In the last chapter we learned that everyone should be doing exactly what they're supposed to do by the book—the procedure manual, that is.

In this chapter, we'll use a budget to establish the metrics that will guide your business into the future. A budget is:

- A roadmap to success
- A goal
- An outline for the company on what each profit center needs to do to make a profit

The budget, which shows the goals you need to accomplish in order to be profitable, reminds me of a story about a dog named Aslon…

When my son and daughter were small, they rode the bus to school. The bus stop was only about a block away, in front of a house where a beautiful collie named Aslon lived. Aslon greeted my daughter every day on her way to school. He was so excited to see her, he would run up and down the fence over and over.

When the bus returned after school, Aslon was as excited as ever and would jump over the fence to see my daughter. He jumped the fence many times per day, on the weekends and during summer vacation. Whenever he saw my daughter, Aslon jumped the fence to be with her.

It made no difference what my neighbor did to reinforce the fence, Aslon still made it over. He had a non-negotiable goal—to be with my daughter.

Aslon's owner finally came to our house one day. She asked if we would take Aslon as our own because she could not keep him away from my daughter. He had escaped and been picked up by the pound too many times to count.

Aslon's goal was realized.

I like to tell this story because no matter what the obstacles were, Aslon was compelled to be with my daughter. He never lost sight of what he wanted. He was focused on his goal and he succeeded.

Profit isn't a desire—it's a mandatory destination. I've seen many business owners go to work without exhibiting a desire (or the ambition) to be profitable. They somehow think that if they go through the motions, profit will drop out of the sky and land in their lap. You must plan to make a profit, and then execute that plan to make a profit.

When I was in graduate school, Sam, my major professor took me to dinner just before my final defense of my dissertation. We were at his favorite Italian restaurant enjoying a delicious dinner and stimulating conversation.

Being that I was a cocky graduate student, I began to spout off about what a great trainer I was. I told Sam that I could train anyone using various tools like e- learning, audio-visual, printed text, workshops, seminars, one-on-one, etc.

Sam just kept eating, letting me carry on about my excellent training skills. After listening to about 10 minutes of this, Sam politely wiped his mouth and said, "Ron, you're a great teacher, but students must want to learn."

That was profound. It set me straight and it should set you straight as a business owner. Do you want to learn? Do you want training to do better? Is profit something you'd maybe like to achieve or is it a mandatory goal? Your attitude can make all the difference in the success of your company and in your life in general.

Be Profitable

All companies must make a profit to exist. When you want to forecast a period of time, like one year, you're making your best guess as to what it will take to make a profit during that timeframe.

The Risk Management Association (RMA) (rmahq.org) prints a useful book showing financial information about different types of companies. You can also access this information online or from a trade organization, but you'll need to know your North American Industry

Classification System Code (NAICS). All businesses have a code for data collection, IRS and financial statistics. Look up the national average profit for your code.

For example, in the heating, ventilation and air conditioning and plumbing industries (NAICS 238220), the average net profit is about 3%. This is the average—many companies exceed 20% and many make a negative net profit. In these industries, the net profit that you want to make is at least 8% after all costs of doing business have been paid and the owner(s) have taken a salary and benefits.

Profitability is what we'll use to project growth and create a budget. A budget consists of:

- Estimated sales
- Costs of sales
- Overhead
- Profit

Most companies start at the top and estimate sales. I'm different (as you may have noticed) and I start at the bottom. It makes no difference what you sell, or what you project to sell, if your profit is zero or less. You need to start with how much you want to make, then work backwards to how much you need to sell to accomplish your profit goal.

Create Your Budget

To start the budgeting process for your company, you need to go away. Go away from the office that is. Take your team offsite and focus on what you're going to do over the next year. Leave the calls and distractions behind. Turn off your cell phone for a focused meeting. Consider bringing in an outside facilitator or consultant to gain a better prospective. Use this time to create your budget and then decide how to implement it.

Use the financial equation:

return on investment for the year = Net profit $ at end of the year / Net worth at beginning of year

We all want a return on the investment of time and assets we put into our business. Is the time, effort and resources in your business worth the return? Or would you be better off selling everything and putting the money in the bank or the stock market?

In a service business, you would probably want a 15 to 20% return (or more) in your business—not the 1% (or less) from the bank. Let's work through an example:

If your net worth is $50,000, then 20% of $50,000 is $10,000, or your profit. If you earned a net profit of $10,000 from your business, you also earned a return on investment of 20% on your net worth of $50,000. Thus, you want to build a budget based on a profit of $10,000.

The next equation is:

net profit $ / net profit % = sales

If your net profit percent wanted is 8%, then $10,000 / 8% $125,000. You need to sell $125,000 in goods and services at 8% profit to generate $10,000 in profit.

Thus, our budget looks like this:

Sales	$125,000	100%
Cost of Sales	???	
Gross Margin	???	
Variable Overhead	???	
Fixed Overhead	???	
Net Profit	$ 10,000	8%

We have the top and bottom, but what about the rest?

Look at your year-to-date (YTD) profit & loss statement and use the percent of sales for each of the costs of sales. That's approximately what you're spending now.

Look at your profit & loss again and use the percent of sales for variable overhead. Both costs of sales and variable overhead vary with sales, so you need to use percent of sales to calculate the actual dollar values.

Finally use actual dollars when you enter fixed overhead. Fixed overhead doesn't vary with sales, so you need to use the actual dollars you spent.

If done correctly, you may find yourself with something like this:

Sales	$125,000	100%
Cost of Sales	75,000	60%
Gross Margin	50,000	40%
Variable Overhead	12,500	10%
Fixed Overhead	36,250	29%
Profit	$ 1,250	1% (not 8%)

You have not reached your budget goal of 10,000 or 8% of sales. You have too little sales and too many costs to get to 8%. So how do you get closer to the 8%?

Make Money in One of Three Ways

In all businesses, and I mean *all* businesses, there are only 3 ways to make money:

- Sell more things
- Cut your costs
- Raise price

We talked about these earlier in the book, but if you want to fulfill your budget goals and get the profitability you want, you need to decide what to do every single year.

Each year, ask yourself questions like:

Do I have the personnel and wisdom to increase my sales?

Is it possible to trim costs from the business?

How much of a price increase can I expect in my given market?

For the above budget, we need an extra $8,750 on the bottom line. What can we do to get that?

Our financial formula is:

profit $ needed / profit % = sales

Let's go through the calculations for our three choices.

How much do we need to increase sales to achieve our $10,000 profit? We need an extra $8,750. $8,750 / 1% $875,000. So we'd need to increase our sales from $125,000 to $875,000, an increase of $750,000 or 600%.

We could cut costs. If our overall costs are 99% of sales (100% profit %) then maybe we can cut our costs 7%. Our profit becomes 8%. 8% of $125,000 is $10,000.

We could raise price. If you need an extra $8,750 on the bottom line and your sales are $125,000, the formula for a price increase is: $8,750 / $125,000 price increase. The increase needed is 7%.

In conclusion, this business has three choices:

- Increase sales 600%
- Cut costs 7%
- Raise price 7%

You should do all three. Start with raising prices, then move to cutting costs and finally, increasing sales.

Exercise

Of the 3 choices for increasing profitability, which one is easiest? Why?

Great businesses do all three each and every year. In which order should you make the changes?

Summary

Create a budget for your company each year. Go away from your business to focus on developing a budget for your company overall and for each profit center.

Once you've created a budget for each profit center, review the profit center budget with the profit center manager and develop their compensation plan.

Be sure your monthly budget considers changes in sales. Sales are not equal each month. Many businesses get most of their yearly revenue in three to four months, so plan your budget accordingly.

Monthly budgets will also reveal about three to four months where you'll make a negative profit. Sales are just not high enough during that time to cover your costs. You should make a profit over a 12-month period, but don't be surprised to lose money some months. In the contracting industry, it isn't uncommon for businesses to lose money from November to February each year.

Treat each profit center like a little company and hand it off to a manager. Monitor the profit center monthly to see if you're ahead or behind on your goals. When a month is completed, add another month so you can always see 12 months ahead.

A FINAL NOTE

I hope you have enjoyed the book and will follow the guidelines that I've laid out for your success. I tried to share with you the key concepts for success that I've seen throughout my 36 years of consulting.

You are your greatest liability, and your business succeeds or fails on your efforts (or lack of efforts). Whatever happens, you are the responsible party.

You can't be all things to all people—you can't wear three hats. You must move from the technician hat to the manager hat to the entrepreneur hat as quickly as possible. You'll never grow your business by wearing the technician and manager hats. The only way to change hats is to hire someone, stand back and let them manage. Don't interfere with the manager. You're the coach, not a player on the field.

Prepare financials every month, including correct profit & loss statements, balance sheets and cash flow statements. Run metrics each month to see if you're moving forward or lagging behind the industry performers.

Cash is king. Control how you spend your money in good and bad times. If you don't have enough working capital, you'll "have lots of land but no cattle," as we say in Texas.

Pricing is the first thing you do in a business, followed by marketing, then sales. Raise your pricing in any business about every six months.

Go to flat rate pricing for everything you sell. Quote jobs and give the customer a firm price. Don't sell hourly. Customers don't like that method of pricing.

Remember Customers for Life and remind customers why they chose you in the first place. If you don't remember customers, they won't remember you.

Hire employees on attitude and skill.

Every day ask yourself, "What could we do better as a company? What can I do better as an entrepreneur?"

Get out of your office.

I've saved my best story for last, and I hope it doesn't ruin my fine reputation.

Interestingly, I was a biology professor before I became a business consultant. At the time of this story, when I was teaching at a college near Dallas, I would take my students on field trips every spring. One of my hobbies originated on one of these trips:

I'm a rattlesnake hunter.

The first weekend of March each year, my students and I would go on a rattlesnake round-up to catch rattlesnakes for antivenom. You catch the snakes and turn them in to the local authorities, who then send them to the poison control center where they capture the venom. The snakes are then returned to the field.

"Ok Ron," you're thinking. "That's a great story for my next cocktail party, but what does this have to do with business?" Ok, ok, stick with me here...

We took a break for lunch in a small town. I pulled my pick-up truck up next to another pick-up truck that was surrounded by a large group of people. In the truck was a "rattlesnake guru." Rattlesnake gurus come to the roundups, talk about rattlesnakes, show off their wounds and mesmerize the audience with their stories. And of course, there's always a cowboy hat on the tailgate to collect tips in exchange for entertainment and advice.

I warned my students about these gurus and the misinformation they spread about rattlers, but I also understood that they were just trying to make a little extra money.

The guru asked us if we had gotten any snakes. I said we had about 60 and he asked if he could borrow one. I flipped a four-footer onto the bed of his truck and he picked it up immediately.

He then told the audience that he was going to do something not many others could do—he was going to hypnotize the snake.

Now this would be interesting.

He took the snake by the head with one hand and by the tail with the other. He looked the snake in the eyes. The snake paid no attention.

Ever so slowly, he slid his hand from behind the snakes' head to under its head and began a so-called hypnotizing chant. The audience was totally engaged and I just knew he was imagining the riches headed his way.

He relaxed a bit, and then it happened. The snake coiled back and struck him right between the eyes! The guru dropped the snake, jumped out of the bed of his truck and ran behind the buildings off to our right.

Suddenly it was a madhouse! The crowd was running and crying, most everyone with an eye to where the guru had disappeared.

While everyone else was panicking, I was looking at the snake. It was headed out of the truck right toward the crowd! I jumped in the truck bed and caught it before it could escape.

One of my students had followed the guru, but returned with no news—the guru was gone.

I settled my students and shepherded them into the café for lunch. No one could eat. We were all upset, and rightly so. If you're bitten by a rattlesnake, you want to put the tourniquet between the bite and your heart to stop the flow of venom. However, putting a tourniquet around your neck probably won't keep you alive!

We stayed inside for 30 minutes, then went out to continue our field trip. I couldn't believe it—across the street walked the guru with his head hanging low. We all rushed across to meet him. The man looked directly at me. Between his eyes was a large purple bruise.

He said, "Boy, this must have been my lucky day. The snake was so close to my head that it didn't have time to sink in its fangs, so it just struck me with its nose."

He continued, "my wife stopped coming here with me over three years ago and my daughter said no to me last year. I've been coming here for over 12 years, but today I am motivated to change my life."

He rode off into the sunset.

I hope it doesn't take a snakebite between your eyes to change the way you do business. You're in control. You make the decisions and only you can change the direction of your business.

Make the commitment today not to just run a business, but to develop a passion for your business today, tomorrow and for the next owner. Onward to great profits!

GLOSSARY

Assets Accounts Payables: Invoices on the balance sheet that you owe

Accounts Receivables: Invoices on the balance sheet that customers owe

Accrued Salaries and Wages: Salaries and wages that are due in the future

Accumulated Depreciation: Depreciation that has accumulated over time

Active Customers: Customers that you have invoiced within the past year

Assets: Items on the balance sheet that you own

Auto and Truck Gas and Oil: Variable overhead expense for gas, oil changes, etc.

Auto and Truck Maintenance: Variable overhead expense for auto and truck maintenance

Autos and Trucks Repairs: Variable overhead expense for auto and truck repairs

Bad Debts: Debts from customers that you are writing off on your taxes

Balance Sheet : Document showing history of company financials since day one

Breakeven: Number that indicates you have covered all costs and overhead

Building: Balance sheet purchase price of building

Capital Stock: Startup capital; money and assets you used to start business

Capitalized: Money you have that is free and useable

Cash: Balance sheet value of cash in checking account

Cash Flow Statement: Statement showing cash into and out of the business over time

Cash Surrender Insurance: Cash value of life insurance policies if cancelled

Costs of Goods Sold: Job costs or MESOL above gross margin line on profit & loss

Current Assets: Balance sheet assets turning into cash within 12 months

Current Earnings: Balance sheet showing current profit or loss from profit & loss statement

Current Liabilities: Balance sheet debt due within 12 months

Deposits: Balance sheet value of deposits for utilities and other services;

refundable

Deposits on Jobs: Balance sheet liability showing deposits for jobs not completed

Depreciation: Profit & loss value showing loss of fixed asset values

Direct Costs: Costs of goods sold, job costs, MESOL; must be billable to job

Dual Overhead Pricing: Strategy assigning overhead to MESO and labor for service companies

Employee Benefits: Benefits for employees

Employee Receivables: Balance sheet value of money owed to you by employees

Equipment: Items purchased that have serial number and warranty

Equipment Expense: Repairs and maintenance to shop equipment

Field Labor: Billable wages from field labor

Fixed Advertising: Advertising that is fixed and does not change with sales

Fixed Assets: Balance sheet assets that lose value over time

Fixed Overhead: Overhead that typically does not change as sales change, e.g., rent

Freight: Shipping costs associated with materials, supplies and equipment

Gross Margin: Sales minus job costs; sales minus costs of goods sold

Gross Margin Multiplier: Method of pricing; 100 / 100 gross margin desired

Gross Profit: Outdated name for gross margin

Inactive Customers: Customers you have invoiced, but more than one year ago

Interest and Bank Charges: Interest on loans, credit card fees and bank charges

Inventory: Items such as materials, supplies and equipment purchased for resale

Job Costs: Costs of goods sold; must be billable to person or job

Land: Balance sheet value of land purchased; purchase price not worth

Leads: Definitive person, place and time for appointment

Leasehold Improvements: Improvements to rental property

Liabilities: Balance sheet accounts showing what is owed by company

Long-Term Liabilities: Balance sheet debt that is over one year outstanding

Machinery and Equipment: Balance sheet fixed asset of machinery and equipment owned

Management Salaries: Salaries to exempt employees of company

Materials: Items in costs of goods sold that do not have serial numbers

MESOL: Materials, equipment, subcontractors, other cost and field labor

Miscellaneous Variable Costs: Small costs on profit & loss that do not need their own account

Net Profit Before Taxes: NPBT; sales costs of goods sold overhead; sales breakeven

Net Worth: Assets minus liabilities; value of company on paper

Non-Customers: Persons who have never bought anything from you

Notes Payable Current Portion: Balance sheet amount owed on a note within one year

Office Expenses: Basic office expenses, e.g., paper, pens, copy paper, staples, etc.

Office Furniture and Equipment: Balance sheet value of furniture and equipment in office

Office Salaries: Salaries for exempt employees in office

Payroll Taxes: Payroll taxes paid on profit and loss

POS software: Point of sale software for retail and service companies

Prepaid Expenses: Balance sheet expenses paid in advance, e.g., insurance, rent, etc.

Profit and Loss Statement: Financial statement; sales statement; shows sales activities over time

Rent Expense: Money paid for rent of building, storage unit, etc.

Reserve for Service Agreements: Balance sheet liability account for pre-paid service agreements

Reserve for Warranty Service: Balance sheet account to set aside money for warranty

Retained Earnings: Balance sheet account showing past years' profit after taxes

Return on Investment: Net profit divided by net worth

Sales Commissions: Bonuses paid to sales employees

Sales Revenue: Total invoiced sales for sales period on profit & loss

Section 179: Accelerated depreciation for fixed assets, but no more than your profit

Shop Supplies and Tools: Shop supplies, tools and equipment purchased for less than $500

SMART Goals: Specific, measurable, agreeable, reachable and timely goal criteria

Startup Capital: Balance sheet value of total money and assets used to start business

Total Current Assets: Total current assets including cash, inventory and accounts receivables

Total Current Liabilities: Total current liabilities including notes, loans, payroll and accounts payables

Total Depreciable Assets: Assets on balance sheet that lose value over time

Total Fixed Assets: Total tangible assets that include depreciable and non-depreciable assets

Total Liabilities: Total debt of company as shown on the balance sheet

Total Long-Term Liabilities: Total debt of company after subtracting first year's debt

Total Other Assets: Intangible assets on balance sheet such as goodwill

Travel and Entertainment: Deductible expenses on profit & loss for training, conferences, etc.

Unapplied Labor: Unbillable field labor wages; shop time

Unapplied Materials: Inventory purchased and not sold but missing; costs of goods gone

Under-Capitalized: Not having enough capital to pay bills

Under-billings: Work in progress; work done, but not able to bill

Utilities: Expenses for electrical, gas, water, utilities

Vacation, Holiday and Bonus: Money paid for vacations, bonuses, holidays, personal time, etc.

Variable Advertising: Turn-off and turn-on advertising

BIBLIOGRAPHY

Fails Management Institute (FMI) Report on Dual Overhead

https://www.fminet.com/fmi-quarterly/article/2015/12/pricing-for-profit/

Oncken, William. (1984). *Managing Management Time.* Prentice Hall

Smith, Ron. (2007). *HVAC Spells Wealth.* Ronald L. Smith

Piscitelli, Tom and John Sedgwick. (2016) *Proposition Selling.* BookBaby

Levinson, Jay Conrad. (2007). *Guerrilla Marketing.* Houghton Mifflin

Gerber, Michael. (1986). *The E-Myth: Why Most Small Businesses Don't Work and What to Do About It.* Harper Business

Blanchard, Ken and Oncken Jr, William. (1999). *The One Minute Manager Meets the Monkey.* William Morrow Paperbacks

APPENDIXES

1   Sample Balance Sheet

2   Sample Profit & Loss Statement

3   EFO Report

PROFIT AND LOSS STATEMENT

SALES	$	%	TARGET
Wholesale			
Retail			
Total Sales			
Cost of Material			
Cost of Equipment			
Cost of Labor			
Cost of Subcontractor			
Cost of Warranty			
Other Costs			
Total Direct Costs			
GROSS MARGIN			
OPERATING EXPENSES			
Variable Overhead			
Advertising			
Auto/Truck Gas & Oil			
Bad Debts			
Equipment Expense			
Freight			
Interest & Bank Charges			
Ins. (Work. Comp/Gen. Liability)			
Office Expenses			
Payroll Taxes			
Sales Commissions			
Shop Supplies & Tools			
Travel & Entertainment			
Unapplied Labor			
Unapplied Materials			
Vacation, Holiday & Bonus Pay			
Total Variable Overhead			
Fixed Overhead			
Advertising			
Communication			
Contributions			
Data Processing			
Depreciation			
Dues & Subscriptions			
Employee Benefits			
Legal & Professional Fees			
Licenses & Taxes			
Repair & Maintenance			
Rent Expense			
Salaries - Office			
Salaries - Officer			
Salaries - Sales/Estimating			
Salaries - Supervisory			
Salaries - Warehouse			
Uniforms and Laundry			
Utilities			
Total Fixed Overhead			
TOTAL OVERHEAD EXPENSES			
NET PROFIT BEFORE TAXES			

Sample Balance Sheet

1	ASSETS		
2	CURRENT ASSETS		
3	Cash..	$	_____
4	Accounts Receivable		
5	Employee Receivables...	$	_____
6	Notes Receivable	$	_____
7	Prepaid Expenses..	$	_____
8	Underbillings (Work in Progress)	$	_____
9	Inventory	$	_____
10	**Total Current Assets**	$	_____
11	FIXED ASSETS:..		
12	Building..	$	_____
13	Office Furniture & Equipment...	$	_____
14	Machinery & Equipment...	$	_____
15	Autos & Trucks	$	_____
16	Leasehold Improvements...	$	_____
17	Total Depreciable Assets..	$	_____
18	Less: Accumulated Depreciation	$	_____
19	Net Book Value	$	_____
20	Plus: Land	$	_____
21	**Total Fixed Assets**..	$	_____
22	OTHER ASSETS..		
23	Cash Surrender Value - Officer's Life Insurance	$	_____
24	Deposits..	$	_____
25	**Total Other Assets**..	$	_____
26	***TOTAL ASSETS***	$	_____
27	LIABILITIES & NET WORTH		
28	CURRENT LIABILITIES:		
29	Accounts Payable	$	_____
30	Notes Payable - Current Portion...	$	_____
31	Taxes Payable	$	_____
32	Accrued Salaries & Wages..	$	_____
33	Overbillings or Deposits on Jobs..	$	_____
34	Reserve for Start-up & Warranty Service	$	_____
35	Reserve for Service Contracts	$	_____
36	**Total Current Liabilities**	$	_____
37	LONG-TERM LIABILITIES:		
38	Notes Payable	$	_____
39	Less: Current Portion	$	(_____)
40	**Total Long-Term Liabilities**...	$	_____
41	***TOTAL LIABILITIES***..	$	_____
42	NET WORTH:		
43	Capital Stock (Startup Capital)..	$	_____
44	Paid-In Capital...	$	_____
45	Retained Earnings (previous years).....................................	$	_____
46	Current Earnings (this year)	$	_____
47	**Total Net Worth**	$	_____
47	***TOTAL LIABILITIES & NET WORTH***	$	_____

Electronic Financial Officer
By FinancialSoft

Financial Analysis Report

For the month ending September 30, 2018
(and the prior thirteen months)

Cooler's Heating & Cooling

North American Industry Classification System (NAICS) = **238220**

Secure Data Encryption by:

v189.854

Cooler's Heating & Cooling

Executive Action Summary

Dear John Cooler,

Here is this month's Profit Gap report. This report covers from September 30, 2017 to September 30, 2018, in monthly periods, with a focus on the last month of September 2018. This Executive Action Summary identifies the top opportunities Profit Gap found from your Manual Entry data in the areas of Cash Lost, Profitability, and other Key Performance Indicators metrics where current results reflect a variance of 25% or more from their goal. We strongly encourage you to review your financial information on at least a monthly basis. Most Profit Gap reports show substantial opportunity for improvement. Please look for additional details in the enclosed report.

CASH LOST
The last period in this report, September 30, 2018, indicates the largest Cash Lost opportunity is Accounts Receivable based on the goal set for Receivable Days, Cooler's Heating & Cooling has $81,955 tied up in collecting Receivables sooner verses your goal. For each day you decrease your Receivable terms with your customers, Cooler's Heating & Cooling will have a positive Cash impact of $11,110. Your Total Cash Lost reflected in this report $157,235

PROFIT
As of September 30, 2018, Cooler's Heating & Cooling`s most significant Profit opportunity is Gross Margin based on the goal set for Gross Margin percentage, Cooler's Heating & Cooling is short of it's Gross Margin goal by $8,549. For each 1% increase in Gross Margin, Cooler's Heating & Cooling will have a positive Profit impact of $3,333. The total Profit Impact found this month was $8,549

OTHER SCORECARD METRICS
Additional Key Performance Metrics (that are not Cash Lost or Profitability) that are greater than 25% from your goals include the following:
* The Quick Ratio is at 0.6. With the goal set at 1.2, your company is 49% away from meeting your goal.
* The Sales to Assets metric is at 3.4. With the goal set at 5.2, your company is 35% away from meeting your goal.
* The Debt to Equity metric is at 5.2. With the goal set at 1.2, your company is 333% away from meeting your goal.

Best regards,

Ron Collier PhD.
President
Collier Consulting Group, Inc.
800-739-9025

Key Performance Metrics

COLLIER CONSULTING GROUP

Cooler's Heating & Cooling

eFO — Electronic Financial Officer

Ratio	Formula	Calculations For Current Month =	Actual Annualized	Two (2) Months Ago 7/31/18	Last Month 8/31/18	Current Month + Performance to Goal 9/30/18	Month-to-Month Trend	Goal	Industry Standard
SHORT TERM RATIOS: Liquidity & Profitability									
Current	Current Assets / Current Liabilities =	1,176,700 / 959,900	1.1	1.1	1.1	1.2	▲	1.6	
Quick	Cash + Accts. Rcv. / Current Liabilities =	604,500 / 959,900	0.5	0.5	0.5	0.6	▲	1.2	
Gross Margin	Gross Profit / Sales =	233,700 / 414,100	46.3%	44.6%	42.1%	56.4%	▲	58.5%	
Net Margin	Net Profit Before Tax / Sales =	159,100 / 414,100	6.4%	4.7%	-3.2%	38.4%	▲	7.9%	
CASH CONVERSION CYCLE ELEMENTS									
Inventory Turn-Days	Inventory X 30 Days / COGS (COS) =	51,300 X 30 / 180,400	10	9	10	9	▼	1	
Accounts Receivable Turn-Days	Receivables X 30 Days / Sales =	531,600 X 30 / 414,100	49	49	55	39	▼	33	
Average Payment Period-Days	Payables X 30 Days / COGS (COS) =	230,600 X 30 / 180,400	39	47	48	39	▼	44	
Cash Conversion Cycle	Inv Days + Rcv Days - Payment Days =	8.6 + 39.0 - 38.9	20	11	17	9	▼	-10	
RATIOS OF: Equity & Assets*									
Sales to Assets	Sales / Total Assets =	999,900 X 4 / 1,175,967	3.0	2.9	2.9	3.4	▲	5.2	
Return on Assets	Net Profit Before Tax / Total Assets =	166,100 X 4 / 1,175,967	19%	12.1%	-2.4%	56.5%	▲	14.0%	
Return on Equity	Net Profit Before Tax / Equity =	166,100 X 4 / 191,167	108%	88.6%	-18.5%	347.6%	▲	58.9%	
Debt to Equity	Total Liabilities / Equity =	984,800 / 191,167	6.3	6.3	6.6	5.2	▼	1.2	
WORKING CAPITAL TURNOVER									
Working Capital Turnover	Annual Sales / Average Working Capital =	3,507,000 / 216,800	22.7	36.4	35.7	22.7	▼	8.0	

Industry Standard — Pointer designates current performance verses industry

10% 25%		25% 10%
Top	Median	Bottom

*NOTE: RATIOS OF: Equity & Assets use last 3 month rolling total annualized for the numerator. This is so near-term changes in the performance to the metric are more pronounced.

More Information

Goal Setting Tutorial

Actual Performance to Goal Key

Better than Goal

≤ 25% away from Goal

Greater than 25% from Goal

Greater than 50% from Goal or **Negative** Value

None Numeric Results

NA: designates the Metric does not have all the information to calculate the metric.

∞*: indicates the denominator in the CCC elements is zero (0) making the result a very large

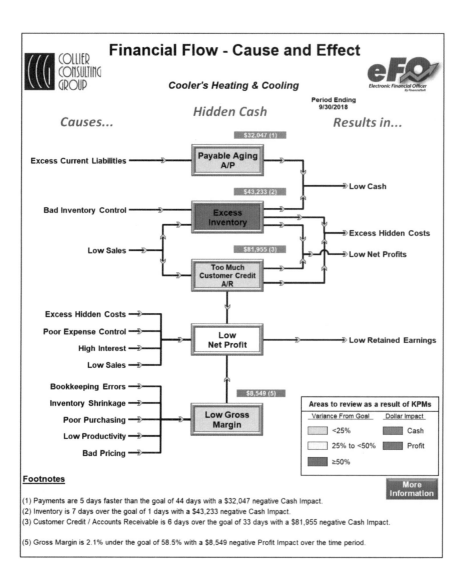

Financial Flow - Cause and Effect

COLLIER CONSULTING GROUP

eFO Electronic Financial Officer *By FinancialSoft*

Cooler's Heating & Cooling

Period Ending
9/30/2018

Hidden Cash

Causes...   *Results in...*

$32,047 (1)

Excess Current Liabilities ———▷ | **Payable Aging A/P** |

▷ Low Cash

$43,233 (2)

Bad Inventory Control ———▷ | **Excess Inventory** |

▷ Excess Hidden Costs

Low Sales ▷

$81,955 (3)

| **Too Much Customer Credit A/R** |

▷ Low Net Profits

Excess Hidden Costs ▷
Poor Expense Control ▷
High Interest ▷
Low Sales ▷

| **Low Net Profit** |

▷ Low Retained Earnings

$8,549 (5)

Bookkeeping Errors ▷
Inventory Shrinkage ▷
Poor Purchasing ▷
Low Productivity ▷
Bad Pricing ▷

| **Low Gross Margin** |

Areas to review as a result of KPMs

Variance From Goal	Dollar Impact
<25%	Cash
25% to <50%	Profit
≥50%	

More Information

Footnotes

(1) Payments are 5 days faster than the goal of 44 days with a $32,047 negative Cash Impact.

(2) Inventory is 7 days over the goal of 1 days with a $43,233 negative Cash Impact.

(3) Customer Credit / Accounts Receivable is 6 days over the goal of 33 days with a $81,955 negative Cash Impact.

(5) Gross Margin is 2.1% under the goal of 58.5% with a $8,549 negative Profit Impact over the time period.

Financial Summary

Cooler's Heating & Cooling
Period ending 09-30-2018

Cash and Profit Impact

Issue	Cash Tied Up	Profit Opportunities
Receivables	$81,955	
Inventory	$43,233	
Payables	$32,047	
Payable Discounts		$4,612.00
Gross Margin		$8,549
Net Margin		
Total	**$157,235**	**$13,161**

Sensitivity Analysis

Metric		Impact
Cash Conversion Metrics		*1-Day Sensitivity**
Inventory Turn-Days	=	$5,683 per day
Accounts Receivable Turn-Days	=	$11,110 per day
Average Payable Payment Period	=	$5,683 per day
Margin Metrics (Month)		*1% Margin Sensitivity***
Margin (Gross or Net)	=	$3,333 per 1%

* Note: A 1 day of improvement in these metrics would increase the
Cash of Cooler's Heating & Cooling by the amount shown based on
the last 3 months average.

**Note: 1% improvement in margin would mean an increase in profits
of $3,333 to Cooler's Heating & Cooling based on the last 3 months
average.

More
Information

Trend Chart
Sales, Net Profit & Operating Cash Flow
Cooler's Heating & Cooling

Sales (Line)

$450
$400
$350
$300
$250
$200
$150
$100
$50
$0
($Thousands)

OCF and Net Profit (Columns)

$150
$100
$50
$0
-$50
-$100
($Thousands)

9/30/17 10/31/17 11/30/17 12/31/17 1/31/18 2/28/18 3/31/18 4/30/18 5/31/18 6/30/18 7/31/18 8/31/18 9/30/18

■ Operating Cash Flow (OCF) ■ Net Profit — Sales (Right Axis)

eFO
Electronic Financial Officer
by Financialsoft

COLLIER CONSULTING GROUP

More Information

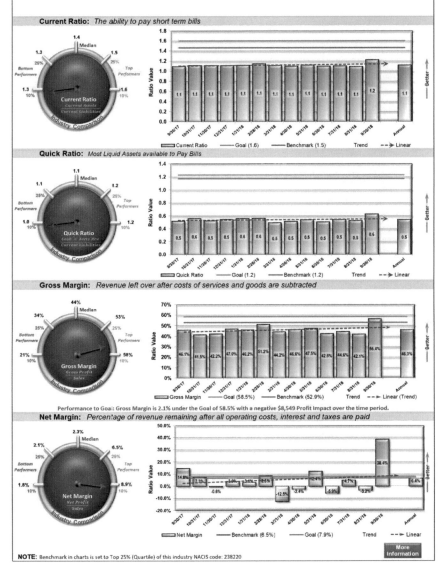

Current Ratio: *The ability to pay short term bills*

Quick Ratio: *Most Liquid Assets available to Pay Bills*

Gross Margin: *Revenue left over after costs of services and goods are subtracted*

Performance to Goal: Gross Margin is 2.1% under the Goal of 58.5% with a negative $8,549 Profit Impact over the time period.

Net Margin: *Percentage of revenue remaining after all operating costs, interest and taxes are paid*

NOTE: Benchmark in charts is set to Top 25% (Quartile) of this industry NACIS code: 238220

COLLIER
CONSULTING
GROUP

eFO
Electronic Financial Officer

Sales to Assets: *How efficiently are you using your assets to produce revenue*

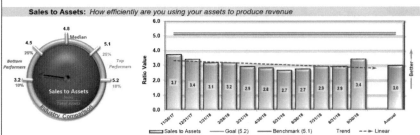

Return On Assets: *Net income generated for each dollar of assets*

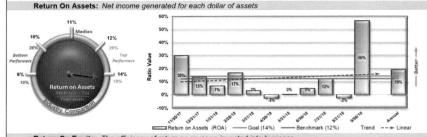

Return On Equity: *The efficiency of return on revenue invested into business*

Debt to Equity: *What is owed compared to Net Worth*

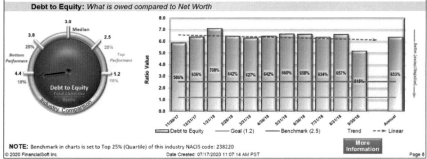

COLLIER
CONSULTING
GROUP

eFO
Electronic Financial Officer

Receivable - Days: *Average time clients take to pay*

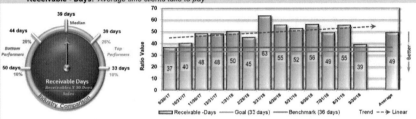

Performance to Goal: Accounts Receivable is 6 days over the Goal of 33 days with a $81,955 negative cash impact.

Inventory - Days: *Average days of inventory or supplies remain in stock*

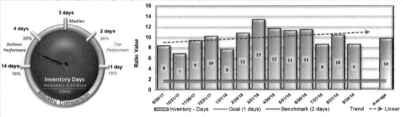

Performance to Goal: Inventory is 7 days over the Goal of 1 days with a $43,233 negative cash impact.

Payable - Days: *Average days to pay suppliers*

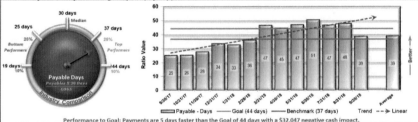

Performance to Goal: Payments are 5 days faster than the Goal of 44 days with a $32,047 negative cash impact.

Cash Conversion Cycle: *Length of time to recapture revenue spent on inventory*

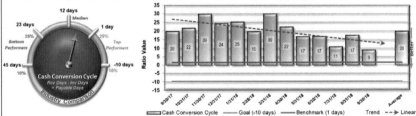

Performance to Goal: The Cash Conversion Cycle is 18 days over the Goal of -10 days.

More
Information

NOTE: Benchmark in charts is set to Top 25% (Quartile) of this industry NACIS code: 238220

COLLIER
CONSULTING
GROUP

eFO
Electronic Financial Officer

Working Capital: *Capital available to operate the business (Current Assets - Current Liabilities)*

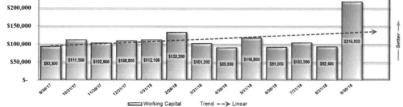

$93,300	$111,500	$102,800	$108,800	$112,100	$132,200	$101,300	$89,800	$116,800	$91,000	$103,500	$92,400	$216,800

Working Capital — Trend ⇢ Linear — Better →

Working Capital Turnover: A company's effectiveness in using its working capital. How many times Working Capital is turned over in 1 year.

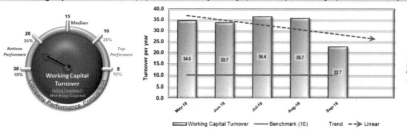

May-18	Jun-18	Jul-18	Aug-18	Sep-18
34.6	33.7	36.4	35.7	22.7

Working Capital Turnover — Benchmark (10) — Trend ⇢ Linear

Days of Working Capital: Number of days of Working Capital remaining if no new sales occur.

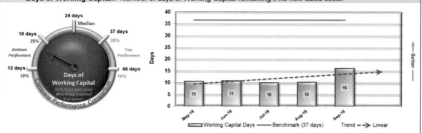

May-18	Jun-18	Jul-18	Aug-18	Sep-18
11	11	10	10	16

Working Capital Days — Benchmark (37 days) — Trend ⇢ Linear

Days of Cash + Receivables to Cover Expenses: Number of days of Cash plus Receivables remaining to cover Expenses if no sales occur.

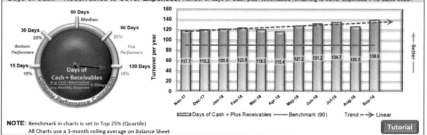

Nov-17	Dec-17	Jan-18	Feb-18	Mar-18	Apr-18	May-18	Jun-18	Jul-18	Aug-18	Sep-18
117.7	119.2	120.6	122.6	119.3	115.4	127.2	131.2	134.7	125.8	136.6

Days of Cash + Plus Receivables — Benchmark (90) — Trend ⇢ Linear

NOTE: Benchmark in charts is set to Top 25% (Quartile)
All Charts use a 3-month rolling average on Balance Sheet

Tutorial

Planning
Impacts of Fixed and Variable Cost Changes
Cooler's Heating & Cooling

Electronic Financial Officer
by FinancialSoft

Sales Required to Support Fixed Costs Changes

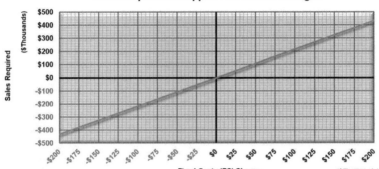

For every $1 FC increase, $2.16 sales increase is needed for same Net Profit.
Formula: Sales Required = $2.16 X Fixed Cost Change
This chart reflects the amount of sales increase that will be needed for various changes in the fixed cost levels in your company.

Net Profit Impact with Variable Cost % Change

Every 1% VC decrease will result in $18,816 of an annual Net Profit increase, correspondingly, every 1% VC increase will result in $18,816 of an annual Net Profit decrease.
Formula: Net Profit Change = -$18,816 X Variable Cost Change (ΔVC)(%)
This chart shows the change in net profit resulting from selected % decrease in your variable cost.

More Information

NOTE: All calulations are based on annualized data, using rolling last 12 months data.

Valuation - EBITDA Method
Cooler's Heating & Cooling

Electronic Financial Officer
by eFinanceable

Net Profit			EBITDA		
Current	6.4%		Current	$	279,000
Top 10% Industry	8.9%		Projected @ Top 10% Industry*	$	387,205

Current Valuation vs at Industry Top 10% Net Profit

▩ Estimated Valuation @ Top 10% of Industry Net Profit performance   ▩ Valuation @ Current EBITDA & Net Profit

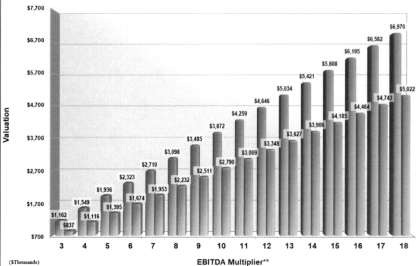

($Thousands)

EBITDA Multiplier**

*Note: This EBITDA estimate scales the company's current EBITDA based on their Net Profit against the top 10% Net Profit of the industry's NAICS code. This is only an estimate as the scaling of Interest, Taxes, Depreciation, and Amortization may not be linear.

**Note: The EBITDA Multiplier can be determined from other recently sold companies in the same industry. This information typically can be found on the Internet or from a Exit Specialist.

More Information

BALANCE SHEET

Cooler's Heating & Cooling

eFO
Electronic Financial Officer
by FinancialSoft

Units: $1,000 ($Thousands)	Ending Period 1 09/30/17	Ending Period 2 10/31/17	Ending Period 3 11/30/17	Ending Period 4 12/31/17	Ending Period 5 01/31/18	Ending Period 6 02/28/18	Ending Period 7 03/31/18	Ending Period 8 04/30/18	Ending Period 9 05/31/18	Ending Period 10 06/30/18	Ending Period 11 07/31/18	Ending Period 12 08/31/18	Ending Period 13 09/30/18
ASSETS													
Cash	$24.4	$38.3	$23.5	$61.2	$57.7	$75.2	$10.8	$22.3	$63.8	$41.3	$27.6	$47.3	$72.9
Accounts Receivable	$492.1	$516.2	$456.7	$455.5	$468.0	$437.4	$435.5	$455.6	$454.0	$437.2	$524.5	$470.0	$531.6
Inventory	$60.3	$51.3	$51.3	$51.3	$38.6	$51.3	$51.3	$51.3	$51.3	$51.3	$51.3	$51.3	$51.3
Other Current Assets	$510.2	$498.9	$491.7	$486.1	$487.2	$480.0	$503.2	$491.9	$511.4	$505.2	$515.0	$506.4	$520.9
Total Current Assets	$1,087.0	$1,104.7	$1,023.2	$1,054.1	$1,051.5	$1,043.9	$1,000.8	$1,021.1	$1,080.5	$1,035.0	$1,118.4	$1,075.0	$1,176.7
Net Fixed Assets	$49.2	$49.2	$49.2	$49.2	$49.2	$49.2	$49.2	$49.2	$49.2	$49.2	$49.4	$49.4	$49.4
Total Other Assets	$76.8	$69.6	$3.2	$3.2	$3.2	$3.2	$3.2	$3.2	$3.2	$3.2	$3.2	$3.2	$3.2
Total Assets	$1,213.0	$1,223.5	$1,075.6	$1,106.6	$1,103.0	$1,096.3	$1,063.2	$1,073.5	$1,132.9	$1,087.4	$1,171.0	$1,127.6	$1,229.3
LIABILITIES & NET WORTH													
Notes Payable - Bank	$438.8	$422.8	$427.6	$437.8	$440.7	$439.4	$439.3	$446.0	$443.0	$440.2	$444.2	$444.6	$482.1
Accounts Payable A/P - trade	$182.6	$191.4	$152.4	$170.0	$164.3	$172.2	$179.2	$196.6	$213.7	$226.5	$278.4	$237.1	$230.6
Other Current Liabilities	$372.3	$379.0	$340.4	$337.5	$334.4	$300.1	$281.0	$288.7	$307.0	$277.3	$292.3	$300.9	$247.2
Total Current Liabilities	$993.7	$993.2	$920.4	$945.3	$939.4	$911.7	$899.5	$931.3	$963.7	$944.0	$1,014.9	$982.6	$959.9
Total Long-Term Liabilities	$34.2	$31.1	$27.9	$24.8	$21.6	$18.5	$15.3	$12.1	$8.9	($1.0)	($1.0)	($1.0)	($1.0)
Total Liabilities	$1,027.9	$1,024.3	$948.3	$970.1	$961.0	$930.2	$914.8	$943.4	$972.6	$943.0	$1,013.9	$981.6	$958.9
Net Worth	$185.1	$199.2	$127.3	$136.4	$142.9	$166.1	$138.4	$130.1	$160.3	$144.4	$157.1	$146.0	$270.4
Total Equity	$185.1	$199.2	$127.3	$136.4	$142.9	$166.1	$138.4	$130.1	$160.3	$144.4	$157.1	$146.0	$270.4
Total Liabilities + Equity	$1,213.0	$1,223.5	$1,075.6	$1,106.5	$1,103.9	$1,096.3	$1,053.2	$1,073.5	$1,132.9	$1,087.4	$1,171.0	$1,127.6	$1,229.3

Date Created: 07/17/2020 11:07:14 AM PST

COLLIER CONSULTING GROUP

INCOME STATEMENT

Cooler's Heating & Cooling

eFO — Electronic Financial Officer

Units: $1,000 ($Thousands)	Ending Period 1 09/30/17	Ending Period 2 10/31/17	Ending Period 3 11/30/17	Ending Period 4 12/31/17	Ending Period 5 01/31/18	Ending Period 6 02/28/18	Ending Period 7 03/31/18	Ending Period 8 04/30/18	Ending Period 9 05/31/18	Ending Period 10 06/30/18	Ending Period 11 07/31/18	Ending Period 12 08/31/18	Ending Period 13 09/30/18
Sales	$407.6	$390.0	$288.2	$288.6	$283.8	$295.9	$209.2	$250.2	$263.6	$237.6	$326.4	$259.4	$414.1
COGS or COS*	$219.6	$228.2	$166.6	$153.0	$152.6	$144.4	$116.8	$133.7	$138.5	$136.3	$180.9	$150.2	$180.4
Gross Profit	$188.0	$161.8	$121.6	$135.6	$131.2	$151.5	$92.4	$116.5	$125.1	$101.3	$145.5	$109.2	$233.7
Expenses													
Marketing, Sales, G&A	$115.6	$120.6	$55.1	$122.2	$120.8	$123.6	$116.4	$120.3	$89.5	$112.2	$127.8	$116.2	$45.3
Depreciation & Amoritization	$0.0	$0.0	$0.0	$0.0	$0.0	$0.0	$0.0	$0.0	$0.0	$0.0	$0.0	$0.0	$0.0
Other Expense	$10.0	$10.0	$66.4	$0.0	$0.0	$0.0	$0.0	$0.0	$0.0	$0.0	$0.0	$0.0	$0.0
Expenses *before Interest & Tax*	$125.6	$130.6	$121.5	$122.2	$120.8	$123.6	$116.4	$120.3	$89.5	$112.2	$127.8	$116.2	$45.3
Operating Profit	$62.4	$31.2	$0.1	$13.4	$10.4	$27.9	($24.0)	($3.8)	$35.6	($10.9)	$17.7	($7.0)	$188.4
Other Income	$0.0	$0.0	$0.0	$0.0	$0.0	$0.0	$0.0	$0.0	$0.0	$0.0	$0.0	$0.0	$0.0
Interest expense	$2.1	$2.7	$1.8	$2.1	$1.6	$2.4	$2.2	$2.3	$3.0	$3.0	$2.3	$1.4	$29.3
Net Profit Before Taxes	$60.3	$28.5	($1.7)	$11.3	$8.8	$25.5	($26.2)	($6.1)	$32.6	($13.9)	$15.4	($8.4)	$159.1
Tax (Income Taxes)	$3.9	$3.2	$3.9	$2.3	$2.5	$2.3	$1.6	$2.3	$2.5	$2.0	$2.5	$2.7	$34.7
Net Profit After Tax	$56.4	$25.3	($5.6)	$9.0	$6.3	$23.2	($27.8)	($8.4)	$30.1	($15.9)	$12.9	($11.1)	$124.4
EBITDA	$62.4	$31.2	$0.1	$13.4	$10.4	$27.9	($24.0)	($3.8)	$35.6	($10.9)	$17.7	($7.0)	$188.4

*Note: COGS=Costs of Goods Sold (Product Business); COS=Cost of Sales (Service Business)

ABOUT THE AUTHOR

Ron Collier, PhD is an author, professional keynote speaker, trainer, business management consultant and entrepreneur. He first entered small business as a training coordinator for a major HVAC and plumbing manufacturing firm. Since 1984 he has been helping small businesses across a variety of industries achieve the profits they deserve.

He has been a speaker at ASBDC (America's Small Business Development Centers), ACCA (Air Conditioning Contractors of America), AHS (American Home Shield), SMACNA (Sheet Metal and Air Conditioning Contractors of North America), PHCC (Plumbing, Heating and Cooling Contractors), QSC (Quality Service Contractors) and other trade organizations, and has led over 800 workshops for these organizations and others.

Ron has helped over 6,000 retail and wholesale companies achieve financial and organizational success through workshops, on-site evaluations, coaching, online webinars and business valuations. He is always focused on a company's profitability and the efficient use of time to achieve maximum success.

His two software programs, Collier Flat Rate (www.collierflatrate. com) and ProfitTracker (www.profittrackersoftware.com) provide small businesses with appropriate methodologies to establish pricing strategies. Ron also represents Electronic Financial Officer (eFO) which automatically monthly accounting data and prepares comprehensive reports and road maps for organizations.

Originally from Texas, Ron graduated from Purdue University in 1983 with a PhD in Instructional Development. He and his wife Sharon have lived in the Austin, Texas area, close to their children and grandchildren, since 2000.

ABOUT RON COLLIER CONSULTING

If your business isn't providing the income and security that you need, in spite of regularly working over 50 hours per week, personal consulting with Ron can get you on the right track.

Using his wealth of experience—he's evaluated 400 businesses, valuated 100+ businesses and spoken to well over 6,000 small business owners—and the knowledge he's gained through relationships with businesses that bring in that bring in anywhere from $300k to over $50M in sales per year, Ron's on-site evaluation of your unique company will take your business where it needs to go.

After a free phone consultation and completion of a Confidential Client Profile, Ron will determine an on-site timeline to help you achieve the profit you deserve. From a one-day visit for small companies to multiple-day visits for larger companies, Ron will thoroughly analyze your current situation and develop a profit plan for your continued success.

Maybe you just need a conversation to see if you are on the right track or a visit to your company for a thorough analysis, Ron provides fresh eyes and new insights into making the profitable company you deserve.

For a free consultation, contact Ron:

ron@collier-consulting.com
Office: 512-858-1670

ABOUT RON COLLIER COACHING

All businesses struggle at times and need an outsider's guidance in running the business. It's incredibly valuable to have a coach with whom you can bounce around ideas and formulate a solid plan for success.

We look at your financials, personnel, pricing and marketing strategies to see if you're headed in the right direction. We monitor you monthly through eFO (Electronic Financial Officer) and set a game plan for your continued success.

Our coaching service will help you run your business through unlimited access to our consulting group via phone, email and video conferencing. We offer one time, monthly and quarterly plans depending on your needs. For a free consultation, contact Ron:

ron@collier-consulting.com
Office: 512-858-1670

BOOK RON COLLIER TO SPEAK
AT YOUR NEXT EVENT

For over 36 years Ron has delivered keynote and corporate meeting addresses, webinars, workshops and breakout sessions to small business owners. From audiences of 2000 or more to small groups of 20 or less, Ron's presentations always focus on profit and the tools necessary to make money for the business.

Known for his humor, stories and experiences with small businesses, Ron can deliver a personalized message to your business owners, franchisees, sales reps, territory managers and dealers. Many business owners can sell and service their products, but most lack the business skills necessary to be profitable. Ron will show them how to make all the profit they deserve.

To book an inspiring and informative speaker for your next event, contact Ron at:

ron@collier-consulting.com

Office: 512-858-1670